MARY JONES AND HER BIBLE

AN ADVENTURE BOOK

Chris Wright

WHITE TREE PUBLISHING

Mary Jones and Her Bible
An Adventure Book
Chris Wright

First published in the United States of America
by Lighthouse Publishing 2009 as
Mary Jones Adventure Book

This new edition © 2011 Chris Wright

Historical characters and incidents are true.
Modern day characters are the product of the author's imagination. Any resemblance to living persons in the story is entirely coincidental.

Scriptures and additional materials quoted are from the *Good News Bible* © 1994 published by the Bible Societies/HarperCollins Publishers Ltd UK, *Good News Bible* © American Bible Society 1966, 1971, 1976, 1992. Used with permission

All rights reserved. Without limiting the rights under copyright reserved above, no part of this publication may be reproduced, stored in a retrieval system, or transmitted, in any form or by any means (electronic, mechanical, photocopying, recording or otherwise), without the prior written permission of the copyright owner of this book.

ISBN 978-0-9525956-2-5

PUBLISHED BY
WHITE TREE PUBLISHING
28 FALLODON WAY
BRISTOL BS9 4HX
UNITED KINGDOM

For my wife Liz,
another Jones from Wales!

Books by Chris Wright for young readers
See back pages for more details

Agathos, The Rocky Island, and Other Stories
Mary Jones and Her Bible – An Adventure Book
Pilgrim's Progress – An Adventure Book
Pilgrim's Progress – Special Edition
Zephan and the Vision

Endorsement

The story of Mary Jones's walk inspired a mission to make the Bible heard.

Today, there are 145 national Bible Societies working with energy and passion in over 200 countries and territories.

Our shared vision is to put a Bible in the hands of those who still wait for God's Word in a language they can understand, in a format they can use and at a price they can afford.

We are delighted that a new audience can read and find inspiration in Mary Jones's story for themselves – thanks to Chris Wright's engaging book. My daughters had a great time as we worked our way through this story and its puzzles.

I warmly commend this fresh and engaging tale to the next generation.

Luke Walton
Culture Audience Manager
BIBLE SOCIETY
Stonehill Green
Westlea
Swindon SN5 7DG
United Kingdom

Introduction

The story of Mary Jones in this book is true. However, the bed-and-breakfast cottage called *Ty'n-y-mynydd* (meaning *Mountain Cottage* in Welsh) is one hundred percent imaginary, as is Mrs Maddox who keeps it. If there is anyone with this name running a B&B in the immediate area, I apologise. However, the things Mrs Maddox says are as accurate as it is possible to be with modern research, and the photographs show the real places and buildings mentioned.

If you go to the area today you will be able to find Mary Jones's cottage, St Michael's Church with the Mary Jones exhibition, the family grave stones, the various monuments, other houses and cottages mentioned here, and in Bala the house and memorial of Thomas Charles. You could even take this book with you and follow the clues, although of course you won't find any hidden pieces of paper!

Remember, you're following in the footsteps of someone famous. Somehow, I think you'll come through this a lot quicker than Mary Jones did!

I would especially like to thank Dr E Wyn James of the School of Welsh at Cardiff University, for his help and support in my research for this book.

Chris Wright

The Adventure Begins

You're going on a short holiday today, an adventure holiday, but so far you have no idea where. You've been busy in the back of your Mum and Dad's car playing games on the video screen, and probably dropping off to sleep from time to time.

You look up. The road signs are not only in English, but also in a language you don't recognise, with *Araf - Slow* written in the road. Another sign says *Man Pasio – Passing Place*. Ahead of you are mountains, and you're puzzled.

You started out in England, and the car hasn't left the mainland. No ferries, just hills and mountains that seem to get higher and higher. So what's this other language? The sat-nav is set for a destination called Llanfihangel-y-Pennant. Your Dad tells you it's south-west of Cadair Idris, the highest mountain around. He doesn't think there are going to be more than five or six houses there. Can you really be on your way to stay in such a remote place?

But discovering where you're going is the easy bit. Soon you'll be facing an assortment of puzzles, and you have to solve them before your holiday is finished.

You don't need to follow the clues or solve any puzzles. You can just read this as an ordinary book. But to get the best from the story, try to solve the puzzles before turning the page. If you're really stuck – and that means *really* stuck – there may be a HINT. Most of the hints are tricky to read, because you wouldn't want to read them accidentally. Would you? If you're *still* stuck, turn the page and the adventure will continue anyway. There's no race to get to the end, so take your time. Of course, if you also speak the language of Mary Jones, a few of the questions will seem too easy – but most of them are designed to be tricky for anyone.

Give yourself two points for solving each puzzle successfully, only one point if you have to read the hint, and nothing for a page where you give up. Sometimes the answers will be for something you've already read on an earlier page. But don't turn back to look. Try to remember.

Here's an easy question and hint to start with, much easier than anything else you're going to find!

what country are you in?

Hint: Look at the back cover of this book!

So this is Wales. You remember from your map of Britain that Wales is a large hilly country joined to the left of England. Even further west is Ireland, but that's across the sea. Hilly? What you can see from the car are mountains, not hills, and you hope you're not going to have to climb every one of them this holiday!

The language on the road signs is something you've never seen before, and it looks as though the place names may be hard to pronounce. Your Dad pulls over and asks a woman walking along the road if there's somewhere to eat round here. "Round here" looks like a pretty bleak place, so there probably won't be anywhere. The woman says yes, and then adds something that sounds just a bit like, "In Mac-hunn-thleth".

The woman is friendly and smiling, and your parents thank her, although you suspect they have no idea what they're thanking her for.

The sat-nav says there are still nearly twenty miles (32 kilometres) to go, and you decide that if you don't eat soon you'll probably starve to death. As you round a sharp bend you see a mountain straight ahead of you that rises up like a massive black wall. Yes, that's some mountain, and it must be near where you're staying.

A road sign says you're entering a town called Machynlleth. This could the place the woman was talking about, but it doesn't seem to be spelt like it sounds.

The Welsh Language

Welsh is a difficult language for English-speaking people to pronounce, mainly because there are letter sounds that the English never use – particularly the double "l". Here is a very quick guide, but to pronounce Welsh correctly you need to be taught – or born in Wales!

"c" sounds like a "k" as in KIT.
"ch" sounds like "kh" in LOCH (a wet "k").
"dd" sounds like "th" as in THERE.
"f" sounds like "v" as in VERY.
"ff" sounds like "f" as in FAR.
"g" is hard-sounding, as in GET.
"ll" sounds like a mixture of "th" and "l" (a hard one, this), with a bit of Welsh "kh" mixed in.
"u" sounds like "ee" as in BEEN, but "au" is pronounced like "i" as in NINE.
"w" sounds more like "oo" as in SOON.
"y" is like "u" as in UNDER, except in the last syllable when it sounds like "i" as in SIT.

There are some exceptions to these sounds, because the pronunciation varies slightly from area to area.

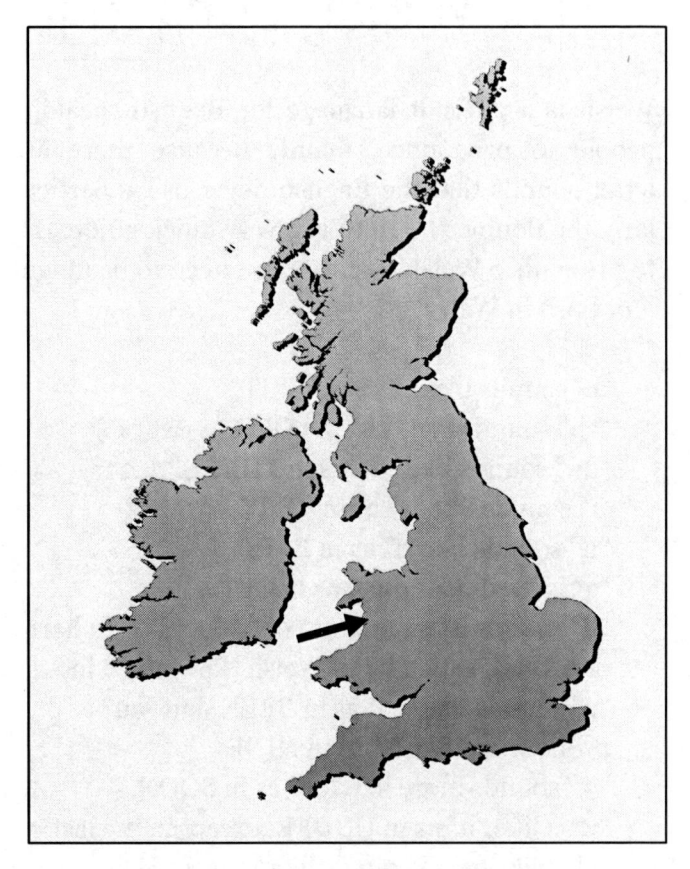

The arrow shows where you are now.

AN ADVENTURE BOOK   CHRIS WRIGHT

Your Dad brakes hard at one of the few parking places by the side of the road in the town. The way he stops makes you think he must be hungry too, which is certainly good news.

You quickly find a bakery selling sandwiches, cakes and drinks. You can eat by the side of the car once you leave town, which suits you fine, as you're anxious to reach your destination. Your Mum says it won't be long now before you arrive.

> What is the name of the village set on the sat-nav? (Don't turn any pages!)
>
> L, L, A, N, F, I, 8, 1, 14, 7, 5, 12 − 25 − 16, 5, 14, 14, 1, 14, 20.

HINT
1 = a, 2 = b, 3 = c, and so on.

The answer is **Llanfihangel-y-Pennant**.

After you've had a family picnic just outside the town of Machynlleth, you reach a village called Abergynolwyn. From here the road is winding and narrow, and the drop to the valley down to the left makes you think you're in an aeroplane. Dad doesn't like heights and Mum asks him if he's nervous.

Dad just laughs and says he doesn't mind – because he's keeping his eyes shut. You look at him quickly, and he seems to be joking. Well, you hope he is, because he's the one doing the driving!

You come to a large valley, and the sat-nav announces that you've reached your destination. The village of Llanfihangel-y-Pennant is indeed small. There's a sign to a campsite, but Mum says tents aren't for her anymore. She's says she has more sense than that. You can't remember when tents were for her, but you're not bothered.

The small cottage Dad stops outside says *Ty'n-y-mynydd B&B* on a small sign swinging from a post that looks like a gallows.

The place seems friendly enough, and your parents tell you they've already booked rooms here several weeks ago, but wanted this to be a surprise. Last week you thought you were going to be spending this Easter holiday swimming in the Mediterranean, so it certainly *is* a surprise!

Mrs Maddox who keeps *Ty'n-y-mynydd* shows you to your room. Your bedroom window looks out over the mountains and a river, and you suspect the water will be too cold for swimming. Not to worry; Mum and Dad suggest you go out and start exploring while they relax by the fire. Yes, it may be spring, but the air is still cold. The wood fire in the hearth of the front room is almost attractive enough to persuade you to stay. But not quite. There are things to discover.

Your Dad calls you back and gives you a piece of paper. "We've come up with something to keep you occupied," he says, laughing. "The answer to this puzzle is extremely tricky, because it won't be the thing you first think of. It's a sort of code."

You study the paper and frown. It looks like an easy riddle. So what's tricky about it? Knowing Dad, you guess he must mean what he says, so you'll look at the wording carefully. This is what you read:

> *Can you see me hiding,*
> *Hiding down the lane?*
> *Up the mountain I am not,*
> *Rather on the plain.*
> *Children maybe here got lessons;*
> *Have you read my first impressions?*

HINT

The first impression is, you're not going to see this.

STOP! **There's no school in this village, so you're wrong if you've been looking for one. Turn back and have another try.**

You can feel pleased with yourself if you're standing outside the church. The "first impressions" are the first letters of each line of the riddle. The lessons that children maybe got here were Sunday school lessons. Your Dad warned you it was tricky!

There's only one church in Llanfihangel-y-Pennant, so this has to be it. The church of Saint Michael. A notice on the small iron gate invites visitors to come in to see an exhibition.

The churchyard is full of graves, and you stop to read a few. Everyone buried here seems to be called Jones. You decide that you could run your own competition, with a prize for the first person to find the grave of someone with another name. But it's not long before you see graves for Williams and Evans.

The church door opens easily when you lift the heavy latch. You go in and start to look round. The inside of the church is lit by stained glass windows, and you see the vestry through the door in the front left-hand corner. It's dark in there, but you find a light switch.

The building has a slightly damp smell, one that you recognise from other ancient country churches. On your left, inside the vestry, is a huge three-dimensional model in a Perspex case, showing the mountains, hills and valleys from here down to the sea. It seems to be made from multi-coloured quilted fabric, laid into the shape of the mountains and valley. It looks really interesting.

Around the walls are pictures and written explanations. Everything is to do with someone who was born here over two hundred years ago.

In a glass case you discover old documents, and copies from various official registers. Some people have signed their names with a cross. Perhaps they couldn't write. But one name keeps cropping up. There's no doubt about it, the exhibition is about her.

What was so important about this person that someone has gone to all this trouble to make an exhibition? It's about a woman – or maybe a girl. Was this her church? Someone would have to be pretty famous to get this sort of treatment. You look again at the things on show.

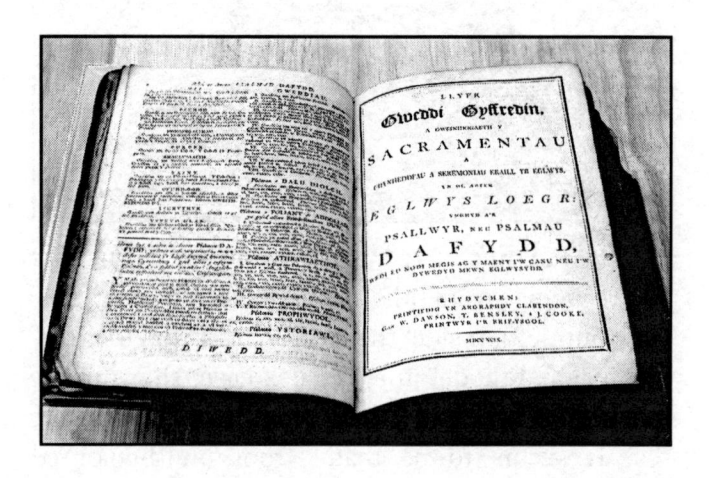

AN ADVENTURE BOOK   CHRIS WRIGHT

Who and what is the exhibition about?

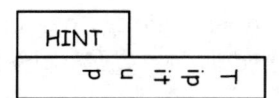

THE HISTORY OF MARY JONES AND BRO DYSYNNI MAP IN THE VESTRY

HINT: push down

The notice says: **THE HISTORY OF MARY JONES AND BRO DYSYNNI MAP IN THE VESTRY**. You may have had a problem with the **BRO DYSYNNI** bit, and just **MARY JONES** will do for your answer. You should have solved that one by holding the page flat, and looking along it from the bottom to the top with only one eye open, almost level with the page.

The Bro Dysynni map is the three-dimensional model filling the long Perspex case, showing the Dysynni river valley from where you are now, all the way down to the sea near Tywyn.

You start to look carefully at the pictures and quickly discover that Mary Jones, the subject of this exhibition, was born in 1784. Her parents married in 1783, so you're not going to find anyone in the village who remembers her – not even Mrs Maddox!

You read that Mary Jones was a Welsh girl who lived just along the road from here, in a cottage called *Ty'n-y-ddôl*, which means *The Cottage in the Meadow*. Mary Jones lived here in Llanfihangel-y-Pennant until she married, but in the year 1800 she did something remarkable, as you'll soon discover.

There's a photograph taken in 1904, showing a crowd of children in front of the remains of what must once have been a house amongst the trees. The caption says: *The Centenary of the Bible Society 1904 at Mary Jones' Home*. Well, you decide, no one can be living in *those* ruins any longer, that's for sure. And you're glad your parents didn't make a mistake with the booking!

You continue to look at the exhibition, and suddenly see a folded piece of paper on the table with your name on it. Your Mum and Dad can't have done this. Someone must be helping them.

The note tells you – and it definitely *is* for you – to go out of the church gate, across to the small red postbox on the wall, and look in the ivy. You are to count how many paces you take between the church gate and the postbox.

You turn out the lights in the vestry and leave through the heavy church door, latching it securely in place after you. The graves mean a bit more to you now, and maybe one of your tasks will be to find the graves of Mary and her parents – assuming they're buried here.

You're enjoying yourself, and this is certainly a holiday with a difference. Maybe you could phone one of your friends back home and say what's happening. You get out your phone, but there's no signal, and you suddenly feel isolated. Well, if Mary Jones could manage without a phone, you decide that you can as well. Maybe you're taking modern technology too seriously.

You wonder what other surprises there are in store for you. You've never really thought about what life must have been like more than two hundred years ago, but you have a feeling you're going to find out over the next few days!

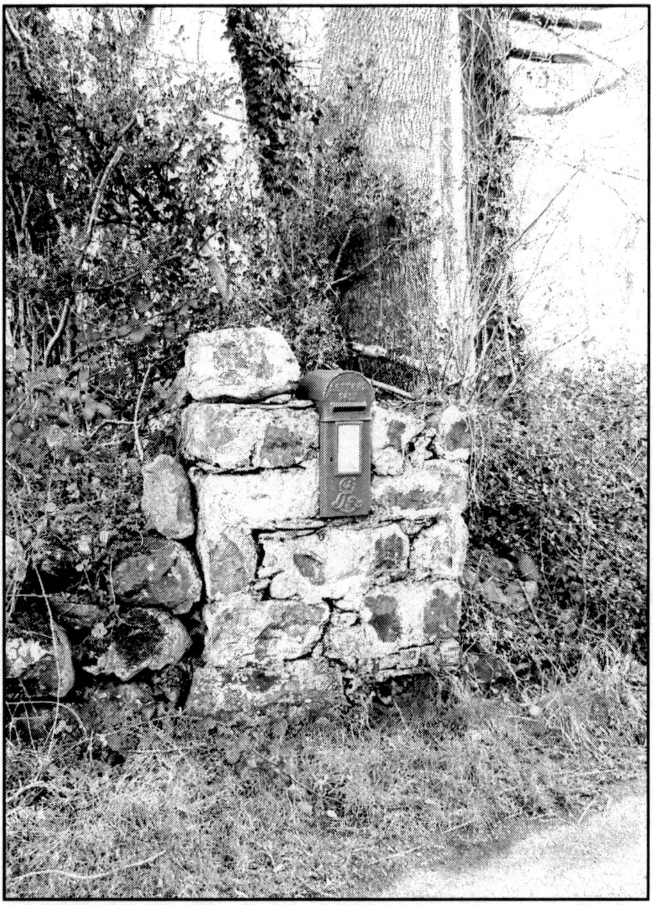

An Adventure Book

Chris Wright

The small red postbox is set in the wall across the lane. You take moderately long strides, and count seventeen. You check in the ivy behind the box, and there is the next piece of paper.

This is what it says:

> Mary Jones was born in 1784.
> Her parents married in 1783.
> The mail is collected at 10:00 am.
> You should have taken 17 paces to get here from the church gate.
> So, how old was Mary when she was born?

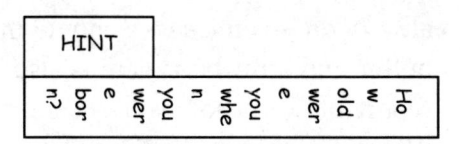

HINT

How old were you when you were born?

Mary, of course, was the same age as everyone when they're born! Someone, probably Mrs Maddox, included the other details to confuse you. There's nothing else you can see in the way of clues. Yes there is. On the other side of the paper you read: *Come back now for tea.*

A small group of walkers pass you, and they look fully prepared to climb Cadair Idris. From here, the mountains seem a little more friendly than they did when you first saw them, but the clouds are covering the tops ready for rain, and you're relieved that Mrs Maddox's house is down here in the valley.

The log fire in *Ty'n-y-mynydd* is still burning brightly in the hearth, and it doesn't look as though your Mum and Dad have stirred since you left. They might even have been asleep. Perhaps they didn't expect you back so soon.

Mrs Maddox has the kettle on – it's probably always on – and serves home-made scones with butter and strawberry jam – also home-made. You report back on how you got on, and Mrs Maddox listens. Somehow she doesn't seem quite as old as she did when you arrived, and certainly won't have met Mary Jones.

Mrs Maddox seems to be something of an authority on the subject. "Did you find the church?" she asks.

You nod, hoping she won't ask if you worked out how old Mary was when she was born! "Can we go and see Mary Jones's house?" you ask.

Mrs Maddox smiles. "It's just along the lane. We'll all walk there when you've had your fill. Mind you, there's not a lot left to see. Just the lower part of the walls. And the fireplace. Goodness, that must have been a *large* fireplace. Of course, we needed fires like that in those days, with no central heating."

We? You wonder after all if Mrs Maddox really was there at the time. Over two hundred years ago? Surely not. But you can't ask her. So instead, you say, "Did Mary live here all her life?"

"Until she married. A harsh life it was, for sure. Her parents were weavers. Welsh wool was a prized thing in those days. Still is. It was a difficult way to make a living, weaving from early morning till night. Mary's poor father died when she was four. He was only thirty. Well, you can imagine how hard Mary had to work to help her mother keep the wolf from the door."

"Wolf?" you say, looking anxiously out of the window.

"Just an expression," your Dad says, laughing.

But of course you knew that, and pull a face. "Any more clues?" you ask.

Mrs Maddox produces a very old photograph of a crowd of children standing around some low walls. "This was taken at the remains of Mary's cottage," she says. "Have you seen it before?"

You remember looking at a copy of this picture. Where was it? You have to think for a moment.

"I saw it in the church exhibition," you say. "It was something to do with a centenary."

Mrs Maddox nods. "You seem to have a good memory. But let's see how good it really is. **In what year was the photograph taken?**"

AN ADVENTURE BOOK   CHRIS WRIGHT

1874?
   1884?
      1894?
         1904?
            1914?
         1924?
       1934?
    1944?
1954?

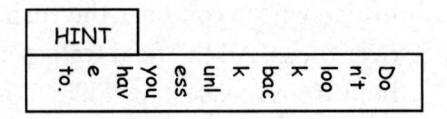

HINT: Don't look back unless you have to.

The photograph was taken in 1904, as part of the Bible Society Centenary celebrations. You remember seeing the date on the copy in the exhibition in the church vestry. Mary Jones's cottage hardly seems worth going to visit – if it was such a wreck in 1904.

Tea is over, and the last scone eaten. Mrs Maddox claps her hands and says it's time for everyone to work off their food with a walk.

You all set out, and soon reach a humpback bridge where you hear the rush of a river splashing over rocks. All the field walls round here seem to be built from rocks shaped like footballs – well, *almost* like footballs. You wonder who could have spent so much time making them round, when square stones would surely be much better.

You see Mary Jones's cottage, or what's left of it, just the other side of the old humpback bridge that hardly looks wide enough for a farm wagon. Two horses are coming over a modern, wider bridge joined to it. The old one wouldn't be able to take the weight of modern traffic. The campsite is nearby, with a sign indicating it's further down the lane.

You look up at the sky, remembering how it had looked like rain when you were leaving the church in Llanfihangel-y-Pennant. Just for a moment, the sun shines through a gap in the clouds, and a low golden light sweeps slowly across the fields and the remains of Mary Jones's cottage.

Underneath the bridge, the river is in full flow from yesterday's rain, with more of these football-shaped rocks littering the river bed. Your Dad jokes that the old bridge must be strong if it took the strain of your weight after all that tea. You look down from it and watch the water crash noisily over the rocks.

"Look at the stones in all the walls and fields round here," Mum says. "They were formed during the last ice age. Geologists say that twenty thousand years ago Wales was covered in ice, probably a mile high in some places. When the ice started to melt, it moved along in huge glaciers, carving out the mountains and valleys under its massive weight."

You point to the walls in one of the fields. "Who made the stones round?"

Your Mum knows a thing or two about geology. She's always been interested in science. "They were rolled around under the moving ice, and in the end they had all their corners rubbed off."

Mrs Maddox is impressed. You wonder if she's ever heard such a thing before. Anyway, the rounded stones wouldn't make very good building material for houses, which must be why they're mostly used in the walls around the fields – even though Mary Jones's cottage has more than its fair share of them.

The chimney of a nearby cottage has white smoke coming from it. The wind has increased now, and maybe it will blow the clouds away and the weather will be fine for a few days. Your father points to the smoke.

"**What goes up the chimney down, but won't go down the chimney up?**" he asks.

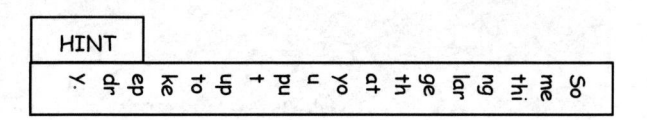

> HINT
>
> Some thing large that you put up to keep dry.

You get the answer in the end, but may have needed a little help – unless you've heard it before. **It's an umbrella**, and the way dark clouds are suddenly coming in from the sea, you guess you may need one soon. The weather seems to change every minute.

Mary Jones's cottage, or what's left of it, has been well preserved, although conservation obviously came much too late in the day. It has been built up – perhaps rebuilt – to around four feet (over a metre) high, leaving much of the end wall intact, where you see the remains of a large fireplace. This must be the one Mrs Maddox mentioned at tea. But with so much of it missing, it's impossible to imagine what it must have been like when Mary Jones lived here.

Although the cottage has some rounded stones in the outer walls, those on the inside have been chipped more or less flat. But you wouldn't want to live in a house with walls like this.

The roof has long gone, so everything is open to the elements. The floor has been recently paved over, and a high memorial stone – the word obelisk comes to mind – in a pinkish red colour rises in the centre.

Mrs Maddox says there's a mistake somewhere in the wording. The lower plaque is in English, but the higher one has the same words in Welsh, except that Mary Jones's name is spelt Mari Jones.

"Is that the mistake?" you ask.

Mrs Maddox shakes her head. "No, that's not the mistake. Mari is the way the name Mary is usually written in Welsh," she explains. "We pronounce it a bit like the word 'marry'. But most people call her Mary Jones with a y, so that's what we use when we're writing about her in English. And it may be how she spelt her name anyway."

The whole idea of the Welsh language is something you've never thought about before. "People don't really speak Welsh here, do they?" you ask.

Fortunately, Mrs Maddox sees the funny side of your question. "Some people might be very offended by that," she says, with a smile. "We have Welsh television, Welsh newspapers and Welsh books. We teach English in our schools, but nearly all lessons are spoken in Welsh. Of course, nearer the English border English tends to be used more widely. But round here I could show you plenty of people who prefer to speak Welsh rather than English."

"I saw some Welsh road signs on the way," you say.

"Ah yes," Mrs Maddox says, "we have to put them in both Welsh and English, because it's official government policy. Did you see the English word SLOW, and a Welsh word painted with it in the road?"

Yes, you remember seeing a few of these signs, and have a feeling you know what's coming next. It's only later that you realize Mrs Maddox didn't tell you what the mistake was on the monument. Perhaps she's planning to tell you soon.

"And what's the Welsh for SLOW?" Mrs Maddox asks.

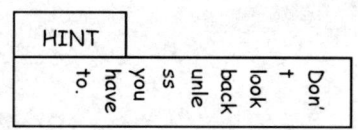

HINT

Don't look back unless you have to.

You remember that the Welsh for SLOW is **ARAF**. Mrs Maddox explains that the letter F is pronounced as a V in Welsh. She says you need two letter Fs together to sound like an English F.

To get inside the remains of the cottage you have to climb up three slate steps jutting out of the wall. They seem to go right through, because as you climb up, you can see three matching ones sticking out on the other side. It's quite an awkward climb, and you hesitate.

"You're allowed to go inside," Mrs Maddox says, perhaps mistaking the reason for your pause.

So you get over quickly, and Mum and Dad follow, although they have to steady each other.

Mrs Maddox stays behind, perhaps wisely, and leans over the wall. "Mary Jones's mother and father were very poor," she says. "I want you to imagine Mary sitting by that big fireplace with her mother, weaving Welsh wool that came from flocks of sheep kept below the mountains. Not their sheep, of course. We can have no idea today just how poor these people were."

This time *you* ask the question! **"Could they read and write?"**

What does Mrs Maddox say?

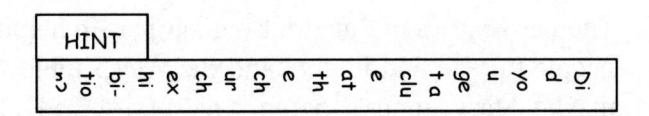

HINT
Did you know that at this time in history, most people could not read or write?

Mrs Maddox smiles in delight, as though she wants you to keep asking questions. Perhaps she does. "There weren't any schools in these remote areas when Mary Jones's parents, Mary and Jacob married. They had to put crosses instead of signatures for their names on their marriage certificate. There's a cross on their daughter Mary's baptism registration that you'll see in the church later, but I think it was put there more recently by someone who wanted to mark the place, and then added the date 1784 at the same time."

"If they had to sign their names with a cross when they married, does that mean Mary's parents couldn't read?" you ask Mrs Maddox.

"Not necessarily. **People could often read even though they couldn't write,**" she explains. "A clergyman called Griffith Jones set up what were known as Circulating Schools in the 1730s. These schools stayed in an area for a few weeks or months, just long enough to help children start reading. Eventually, they closed down altogether. Soon after Mary Jones's parents married, the Rev'd Thomas Charles of Bala took a great part in helping people to read and understand the Welsh Bible. So maybe Mary Jones's parents learnt to read and write then."

"That's Thomas Charles's name on the memorial at Mary Jones's cottage," you say, glad that you've been making good use of your eyes and memory. "I saw his picture in the church. Something about supplying Welsh Bibles. Didn't people have Bibles in those days?"

"Very few. You've no idea how expensive Bibles were. If I told you that a Welsh language Bible from the town of Bala cost three shillings and sixpence in 1800, would that sound cheap or expensive?"

"That's seventeen and a half pence in today's money," your Dad whispers. "Not nearly enough for even a small bar of chocolate."

"So it was almost nothing," you say in surprise.

"Back then it wasn't almost nothing," Mrs Maddox says, laughing. "But it was extremely cheap for a Welsh Bible. These were from a special printing done in Oxford in 1799. Until then, a Welsh Bible could have cost you five or even ten times that price. Of course, very few things were bought and sold out in the country. They were exchanged, because people simply didn't have money to spare. That's why it may have taken Mary Jones six years to save up for a Bible."

> Mary needed three shillings and sixpence for a Bible. There are twelve old pennies in one shilling, and a sixpence (six pennies) is half a shilling. If she saved up for six years, how many old pennies would Mary Jones need to save each year?
> (No hints for this, but if you use a calculator you only get one point.)

Did you get an answer of **seven old pence a year**? Well, you should have done! There are forty-two old pennies in three shillings and sixpence – 36 plus 6 gives 42, divided by 6 (for the years).

You climb back over what's left of the cottage walls and walk down to the noisy river crashing over the rocks. Your Mum and Mrs Maddox join you. Something is puzzling you.

"So where did Mary learn about the Bible?" you ask, thinking perhaps you should have spent longer at the exhibition in St Michael's Church.

"When Mary Jones was young there was a lot of bad feeling between the Anglican Church and chapel folk," Mrs Maddox explains. "It took a long time for it to die down. Anyway, the local Methodists ran a seiat, or midweek fellowship meeting, where members could talk about their Christian faith and receive help and teaching from the Bible. Everyone would have been encouraged to read the Bible for themselves."

"Would children have gone to the seiat?" you ask.

"Not usually," Mrs Maddox says. "But for some reason, we don't know why for sure, but it may have been her eyesight, Mary's mother wanted company on the walk to the seiat after Mary's father died. Mary went with her, holding the lamp when it was dark. I'll show you the farmhouse the Methodists went to in the woods for their seiat. It's only a ruin now."

"So that's when Mary would have heard the Bible being read," you say. You have a vision of Mary going on ahead with a powerful flashlight, but of course that can't be right.

"Just a candle, or maybe an oil lamp, held inside a metal framework, with a window in the front made from a piece of cow's horn shaved so thin that the light could shine through without the flame blowing out on a windy night."

You've not been here after dark yet, but you can imagine it would be pitch black if the clouds covered the moon and stars. Just a candle shining through a thin piece of cow's horn? A girl who could only save a few pennies a year? What on earth was it like living in the late 1700s?

When you examine the remains of the cottage from the riverside, the noise of the river makes talking difficult. "I don't suppose they had double glazing in those days," you shout.

Mrs Maddox shakes her head. "I doubt if they even had glass," she says loudly.

"So how could anyone find their way around indoors if they didn't have windows?" you ask.

"Oh, they had windows," Mrs Maddox explains, coming closer, "but poor people like Mary's parents couldn't afford to put glass in them. To keep the wind out on cold days and nights they hung up wooden shutters. I don't suppose the shutters did all that much good in some of the winter winds we get here."

Your Mum shivers. "How could the family see to do their weaving?" she asks.

You frown, and in your mind you picture all sorts of different lights. Then you start to wonder which of these the family could have used indoors when Mary was young.

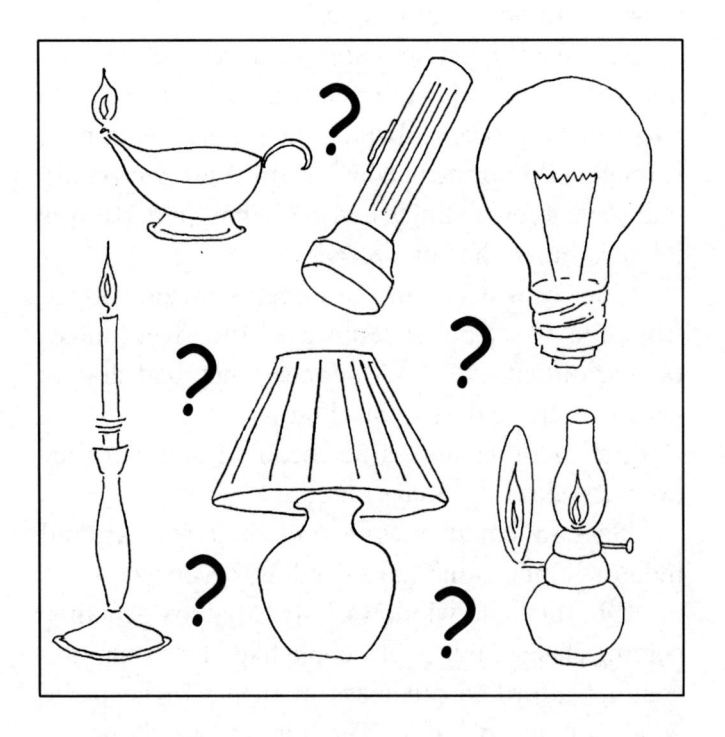

You decide not to ask if they had electricity, but wonder if perhaps they had gas lighting. No, that couldn't be right. Even today, there are places out in the country that don't have a gas supply. But it must have been something with a flame.

Mrs Maddox writes on a piece of paper. "This is what they generally used," she says, giving it to you.

The letters are jumbled up. **What does it say?**

CHALTDINGLE

HINT: The two words start with C and H.

You rearrange the letters and the answer is **CANDLELIGHT**.

Mrs Maddox explains that oil lamps and even candles were so expensive that poor people like Mary's parents would only use them when they really had to. Everyone would get up as soon as it was light, take down the shutters and work until it was too dark to see in the evening.

"They had the big fire," she says, "and there was plenty of wood and peat for burning. But with no proper windows to keep out the wind and rain, they must have got dreadfully cold. I've read that the winter after Mary's parents were married was one of the coldest ever recorded. It was so cold that the sea froze at Towyn. I don't know how anyone survived."

Your Mum knows something about this. She explains that a massive volcanic eruption in Iceland in 1783 covered most of Europe with a huge cloud of ash and poisonous gas. The winters were severe for several years afterwards. "You see paintings of people skating on big rivers like the Thames," she says. "It was a mini ice age. Instant climate change. Lots of people died because of the poisonous gas from the volcano, and many of the people who survived the gas died from the cold."

"It must have been really hard for Mary's parents to stay alive," Mrs Maddox says. "Mary was born just before Christmas a year later, in 1784. I've often wondered how they managed to keep their daughter's tiny body warm in this cottage at the best of times."

Your Mum seems to be shivering again. You climb down the river bank and put your hand in the water. It feels absolutely freezing! "I don't think I'll bother with swimming," you say.

Mrs Maddox laughs. "That water comes straight off the mountains. Believe me, it's a lot warmer now than it is in the middle of January. I've seen this river frozen solid some winters."

The large fireplace has mostly gone now, but you can see the end wall of the cottage where it used to be. So this is where Mary grew up. You try to imagine the family working here in subzero temperatures.

"Mary's father Jacob died when Mary was only

four years old," Mrs Maddox says. "I'll show you his grave in the churchyard later. From then on, Mary had to work around the cottage while her mother tried to make ends meet with her weaving. Life was hard, and manual workers didn't have any money to spare for little luxuries."

You get an amazingly clear picture of Mary's mother working in front of the fire, with Mary out gathering firewood just to keep them both from literally freezing to death in the long, dark winters.

Your Dad is collecting short lengths of sticks. You wonder if he's going to take them back to *Ty'n-y-mynydd* for the fire, but he's hiding them at the end of the cottage. He's obviously up to something, but you don't like to ask what. It's probably to do with the adventure.

"Can you remember the name of Mary's parents?" Mrs Maddox asks. "And this isn't one of the special puzzles."

You wonder whether to say, "Mr and Mrs Jones," but that won't be a good enough answer. Then you remember. "Mary and Jacob," you say. "But wouldn't it have been confusing to have two Marys?"

"I expect there was some special name her husband used, to distinguish his wife from their daughter," Mrs Maddox says. "In her 1882 book, Mary Ropes wrote that Mary's mother was known as Molly, but I don't think there's any evidence for that."

Your Dad stretches, as though he's had a busy day. "Mum and I are going back to *Ty'n-y-mynydd* cottage with Mrs Maddox," he says, "but I want you to stay here. I have a puzzle to keep you occupied, and don't come back until you've solved it. And you'd better solve it quickly, or you'll miss your evening meal!"

He hands you yet another piece of paper.

TAED NAKC ABEM OCOD

HINT: Write the letters out backwards.

You remember that codes are often written with the letters in blocks of four, so no one can guess any words by how long or short they really are. Reading it backwards with no spaces the message says:

DOCOMEBACKANDEAT

which of course is **DO COME BACK AND EAT**. The fresh mountain air is making you hungry again. All that time wasted, and you could have been sitting down to a meal by now!

After your meal, the rain starts to hammer down. Cadair Idris and the other mountains have completely disappeared in the low clouds, and you know you won't be going out again today. You wonder what's happening to the river behind Mary Jones's cottage, and even more, what's happening at the campsite beyond the cottage.

Mrs Maddox asks you to come over to a large table where she has laid out all sorts of bits and pieces. There's a sheet of paper with various dates on it. You're not always interested in historical dates, but this is different. Mary Jones was a real person, and she lived right here in the village of Llanfihangel-y-Pennant, surrounded by mountains.

You already know that Mary was born just before Christmas in 1784, but you know almost nothing about her after that – except that she bought a Bible!

Mrs Maddox says that Mary's parents were Christians who loved God and wanted to find out more about the Lord Jesus. After Mary's father died, Mary and her mother continued to go every week to *Y Llechwedd*, a farmhouse in the woods near the church. It was there that a Methodist preacher called William Hugh – or Pugh – held the midweek seiat. The seiat, Mrs Maddox explains, is where Mary had to carry the lantern for her mother on dark nights.

"Mary wanted to read the Bible for herself, but she couldn't read. She had to wait until Thomas Charles opened his Circulating School two miles away in the village of Abergynolwyn."

That's about three kilometres. "We came through there," you say. "It was the other side of the steep mountain road that Dad didn't like driving on."

Mrs Maddox says, "Well, Mary's teacher also started a Sunday School in Abergynolwyn. Mary was one of the keenest pupils at both schools, and it wasn't long before she was able to read the Bible – in Welsh, of course."

"But she didn't have a Bible of her own at that time," your Dad adds. He can't resist showing off. "When she was about ten, Mary started walking once a week to a farmhouse nearly two miles away to read the Bible there."

"**Do you know the name of the place?**" Mrs Maddox asks you both.

You have no idea, and your Dad shakes his head, probably wishing he'd kept quiet. "You'll have to tell us," he mumbles.

"Some people think Mary walked to the farm high on the hills called **Penybryniau Mawr**, meaning something like *Great Hilltops*." Mrs Maddox says it quickly, to save your Dad any further embarrassment. "*Penybryniau Mawr* is no longer standing, and it may be where Mary was born. Other people reckon she walked to **Bodilan-Fawr**, down here in the valley. That name means *Ilan's Large Dwelling*. Wherever it was, Mary said later that she was allowed to read the farmer's Welsh Bible there – as long as she took her clogs off before going indoors!"

Mrs Maddox explains that Welsh clogs looked like ordinary leather boots and shoes, but they had wooden soles and heels with metal studs.

"Here's a picture of the farm at *Bodilan-Fawr*," she says, showing you a photograph of a mountain.

At first, it's hard to see the farmhouse. But there it is, hiding at the bottom of the picture, in the centre.

"Now then," Mrs Maddox says, "here's a puzzle, but it's not one of your father's tricks. There's a Bible that came from *Penybryniau Mawr* with an old note written inside saying that it's the one that Mary Jones read."

"Then she *did* walk to *Penybryniau Mawr* on the top of the hill," you say.

Mrs Maddox shakes her head. "Not necessarily. Maybe the people at *Bodilan-Fawr* passed it on to the family at *Penybryniau Mawr*, because some people believe that Mary had relatives up there."

"Very confusing," you say.

"Very," Mrs Maddox agrees. "Let's see if this also confuses you. This is the date of the Bible that had the old note inside. It was printed in **MDCCXVII. What date is this?**"

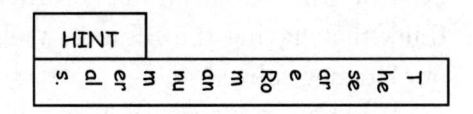

> HINT
> There are Roman numerals.

MDCCXVII is 1717. In Roman numerals, M is 1,000, D is 500, C is 100 (there are two of them to add together), X is 10, V is 5, and finally there are two I's, both of which are the number 1. Add them all up and you get 1717.

"Mary walked to the farmhouse every week," Mrs Maddox says, "just to study that Welsh Bible, because she couldn't take it home with her. She spent much of the time learning parts of it by heart, but her dearest wish was to have a copy of her own."

"Seventeen-seventeen," you say thoughtfully. "That sounds old. When did the Bible first get translated into Welsh?"

"In 1567 Richard Davies and Thomas Huet helped William Salesbury to translate the New Testament and Psalms. In 1588, William Morgan translated the rest of the Bible into Welsh, and it was revised in 1620. It's known as William Morgan's translation, and some people still use modern copies of it today. William Morgan used words that were considered old fashioned even in 1588, because he thought it made the book seem more poetic and majestic. In some ways it's like the English King James Bible of 1611. Many people think that having the Bible in Welsh is what kept our language alive."

"Did any shops round here sell Welsh Bibles in Mary Jones's time?" you ask. "You know, to anyone who had enough money."

Mrs Maddox shakes her head. "Shops? There weren't any shops around here. There must have been pedlars and the occasional market fair, but they wouldn't have sold Bibles. Bibles in the Welsh language were in extremely short supply, but English ones were easier to get, and cheaper. But very few people around here spoke English, and certainly Mary Jones didn't."

"Is this what this adventure is all about?" you ask. "Discovering how Mary got her Bible?"

"It certainly is," Mrs Maddox says. "There's something remarkable about Mary's story. She was eight when she gave her heart to Jesus and trusted him as her Saviour. Then as soon as she learnt to read, she decided to save up for a Welsh Bible of her own. She didn't know where to buy one, and anyway she had no money. **I told you when we were down by Mary's cottage how much a Welsh Bible cost in 1800. Can you remember how much it was in old shillings and pence?"**

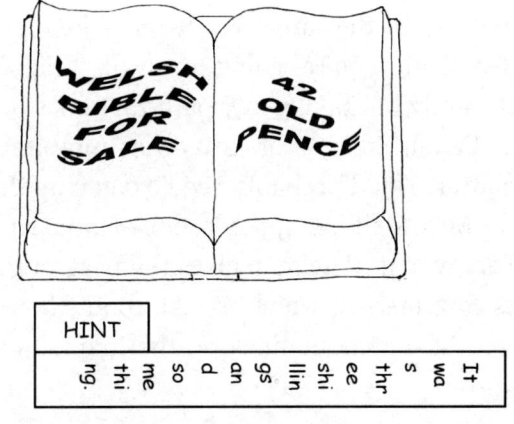

HINT: It was three shillings and some pence.

The answer is three shillings and sixpence – seventeen and half pence in modern money, or as your Dad said earlier, not nearly enough to buy a small bar of chocolate today. But of course, money was worth much, much more in those days.

Mrs Maddox shows you some maps of the area on the table, and you find the various towns and villages that she's mentioned. The sea isn't far away, and the coast is marked with lots of sandy beaches. The water there would be a lot warmer for swimming than the icy river, but only in the summer.

"Are you ready for your walk?" Mrs Maddox asks.

"Walk?"

"To Bala."

"Is Bala close?" you say.

Mrs Maddox smiles. "It's a twenty-six mile trek."

A twenty-six mile trek? That's over forty kilometres! In the rain? Surely she's joking. Well, you decide, if you're going to walk that far, you're certainly not taking any path that goes over the top of Cadair Idris – or any other mountain for that matter. You'd probably need oxygen up there!

Mrs Maddox spreads out a modern Ordnance Survey map. The map gives the peak of Cadair Idris as 893 metres, which is just about three thousand feet. The contour lines on the map show just how steep it is. Well, you don't need the map to tell you that – you've already seen it!

Mrs Maddox leans over and points to where Cadair Idris is marked. "Idris Gawr was a legendary local king, but some people believed he was a giant who lived on the mountain. **Can you guess what *Cadair* means?**"

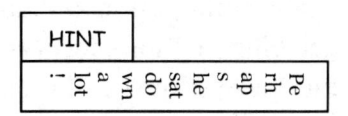

> **HINT**
>
> Perhaps he sat down a lot...

"The name means **Seat, or Stronghold, of Idris**," Mrs Maddox explains.

"Do you think Mary Jones ever climbed up there?" you ask.

"It's unlikely. Mary was too busy helping keep the wolf from the door." Mrs Maddox seems fond that expression. "Anyway, I don't suppose anyone around here would have found the time to go gallivanting up mountains. Ordinary people didn't go climbing for sport back then. If you want to try it, make sure you're properly prepared, and follow the known routes." And she shows you an old picture of Cadair Idris.

An Adventure Book — Chris Wright

No, you don't think you'll bother climbing it. Not just now, anyway.

At last it's time for bed, and it's been a long and exciting day. You take a quick look out through the front door into the night, and discover it's raining hard. You wonder if the rain will spoil your adventure tomorrow.

Before you go to bed, your Dad gives you another clue, but says you're not to go outside looking for the answer until the morning. There's nothing to stop you reading it tonight, and trying to solve it before going to sleep. You keep reading it aloud until you feel drowsy, and the meaning seems to change.

> *This is for people*
> *With feelings intense;*
> *Mums who don't like it*
> *Say they've more sense!*

HINT

Read the two words in the INTENSE logo upside down.

You lie in bed saying *intense* to yourself, until you imagine you're saying *in tents*! And that may not be as silly as it sounds. **You remember the sign to the campsite just down the lane.** And who doesn't like camping and says they've more sense? Your *Mum*, for starters!

As soon as it's light you creep out of your room, down the stairs, and let yourself out of *Ty'n-y-mynydd*. The morning sky is clear pink and blue, and the wet road glistens in the morning light. It seems to have rained a lot during the night, so probably the river behind Mary Jones's cottage will be even more noisy today.

Before you go to find the campsite, you stop for another look at the remains of Mary Jones's cottage. Your imagination isn't quite up to seeing

Mary and her mother going in and out. Even so, the countryside probably looks much the same as it did when Mary lived here.

The doorway was filled in when the lower walls were restored. You climb into the cottage and stare at the remains of the large fireplace, the top of which is covered in dark green ivy. It becomes easier now to imagine life here two hundred years ago. Mary running in with firewood or blocks of dried peat to keep the place warm, and her mother sitting in the gloom, weaving wool from early morning until night. No, to be honest, you can't imagine what life was like before electricity, television, phones and computers – and no Bible.

You climb back into the lane, feeling that perhaps in some small way you've shared life with Mary Jones – just for an instant. The memorial says Mary *"walked from here to Bala, to procure from the Rev'd Thomas Charles BA a copy of the Welsh Bible."* And Mrs Maddox hinted that you're going to make that journey!

At the far end of the cottage you notice the walls of another building joined to the cottage. It may have been an outhouse or even a pen for an animal. You wonder if it was there in Mary's time. So much history has been lost, so who can tell?

You remember why you've come down here so early. You have your piece of paper with the clue from last night, and you're sure it's something to do with the nearby campsite.

Mary Jones and Her Bible

Mary Jones had to carry the lantern when she went with her mother at night to the seiat in the farmhouse in the woods at the top. Find your way there quickly from Mary's cottage at the bottom, without getting lost.

Across the road from Mary Jones's cottage there's a sign to the campsite. And there, tucked just below the sign, you spot a piece of rolled-up paper that's very soggy. Your Dad must have put it there yesterday, when you were down by the river freezing your hand off.

You think it would be fun sleeping in a tent, but with the heavy rain last night, Mrs Maddox's cottage seems a much better option for now. You feel like hurrying back there for breakfast, but first there's a new puzzle to solve.

You unroll the wet paper carefully, and it's another of your Dad's riddles.

> *I carried too much,*
> *My back felt the strain:*
> *It all happens under me*
> *When we get rain.*

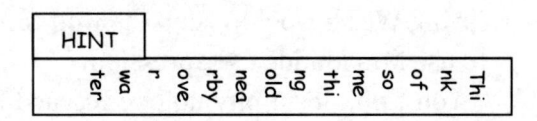

HINT
Think of something nearby over water

You go to **the old humpback bridge** and watch the river, swollen from last night's rain, rushing underneath in a noisy torrent. This, of course, is where you decide the riddle is telling you to go. The old bridge must have felt the strain, which is why the new bridge has been added.

The sound of the water crashing over the boulders makes it hard to think. Last night you thought it would be fun to live with a river outside your window, but now you're not so sure. In fact, everything you learn about Mary Jones makes you realise how difficult life was for country people in those days. Perhaps there was no window on the side facing the river, although the need for light might have been more important than keeping the noise down indoors.

You look across at the remains of the cottage. What is left of the far end wall is slightly higher than what's left of the rest of the building. This is where the large fireplace was. Again, you try to picture Mary and her mother, this time sitting there on freezing days, their fingers stiff with the cold, weaving Welsh wool to keep the wolf from the door – to use Mrs Maddox's expression.

You think it's a pity no one rescued the cottage earlier, while it still had its main walls standing. Of course, farmers and builders would have found a deserted building a handy source of stone as soon as the place was abandoned. Surely people nowadays have much more regard for their heritage

– well, you hope so.

You search around for your next clue and can't see anything in the way of paper. Then you notice a series of arrows made out of sticks. They lead you towards the near corner of Mary Jones's cottage, where you find another piece of rolled up paper. It's also soggy. You wonder if your Dad walked here in the rain late last night. If he did, he must have got soaked. But at least you know why he was collecting those sticks.

The day is bright and clear now, and the clouds have long gone. You unroll the piece of paper.

> *If Mary had been using one of these, this is where she would have had trouble putting it down!*

HINT

Something to do with a chimney.

You remember your Dad's riddle about the umbrella: What goes up the chimney down, but won't go down the chimney up? There's no longer a chimney, but the next clue could be hidden in the old fireplace.

It is. Ivy is hanging over the wall, and you can see something white behind it. Just before you are able to rescue it, you hear Mrs Maddox calling you. She's standing on the old bridge, and comes across as soon as you wave.

"What did this cottage look like when Mary Jones lived here with her mother?" you ask.

"No one can say for sure." Mrs Maddox leans on the remains of the cottage wall, but doesn't climb the slate steps. "Down near Cardiff there's a folk museum in a place called Saint Fagan's. They have rebuilt lots of old houses in the grounds, taken from all over Wales. Stone by stone."

"Didn't the people living in them mind?" you ask, smiling to make sure Mrs Maddox realises you're joking.

She laughs. "They rescue buildings that are either derelict or going to be demolished for new roads. And a marvellous job they're doing. They have a slate miner's cottage that came from a little further north of here, but it's built of the same round stones as Mary's cottage."

You ask if people can go inside it.

"Indeed they can," Mrs Maddox says. "I like to think it's the same as this one used to be. The inside has been furnished, just as it would have been two hundred years ago. There's no ceiling. The room is open right up into the underside of the roof. Just a single room with a fireplace at one end, exactly like here. There's a wooden screen just inside the door, to shield the area around the fireplace from draughts. That would have been where Mary's parents worked before she was born, and later where Mary worked with her mother after her father died."

Mrs Maddox says she has an interest in old Welsh cottages and has made sketches of some of the local ones that she'll show you after breakfast. Breakfast? No wonder you're feeling hungry!

You ask Mrs Maddox where everyone slept if there was no upstairs. She writes this down:

MROFTALPNEDOOWHGIHA

HINT
s tfa t rh et ga e n p

Mrs Maddox points to the end opposite the large fireplace. "There would have been **a high wooden platform** there, standing on the downstairs floor, with the beds on it. You go up a wooden ladder to bed. Not very safe, I'm sure, but there were more dangers to be worrying about than that. Anyway, how about some breakfast?" And for some reason she winks as she says it.

"I've got another clue to solve first," you say, pulling a piece of wet paper out from the ivy.

This one is a real puzzle. There's a large puddle in the lane. You have a feeling that the puddle may help you solve it.

AN ADVENTURE BOOK   CHRIS WRIGHT

How about some breakfast?

HINT
Try using a padded mirror.

The writing is in reverse, so you need a mirror to read it – but a puddle will probably do. **HOW ABOUT SOME BREAKFAST?** No wonder Mrs Maddox winked as she said those exact words. Yes, she admits, your Dad has put her up to setting many of these clues. She arranged for some to be in place before you arrived in Llanfihangel-y-Pennant, and others she's been putting out in the meantime.

"It was rather wet last night," she admits, "but I had to go to the farm anyway, and I had a good waterproof on."

So your Dad didn't get wet, after all. Back at her house, *Ty'n-y-mynydd*, Mrs Maddox shows you a sketch of an old cottage that she says is probably like Mary Jones's house.

Mrs Maddox also has one of a typical interior, showing a large fireplace. You think it's really good

– a sort of window into the past, but you feel sad that Mary's cottage was allowed to get into such a bad state before attempts were made to preserve it.

"Mary's parents were really poor," Mrs Maddox says. "The slate miners who lived in cottages like this further north would have been fairly well off. I don't think *they* would have needed six years to save up for a Bible."

While she's getting breakfast ready, Mrs Maddox lends you a very old book on Mary Jones, written in 1882 by someone called MER. Mrs Maddox says MER was Mary Emily Ropes. Mrs Maddox also has a later edition published in 1894, and in this one you find a picture of Mary Jones's cottage, *Ty'n-y-ddôl*. It was a ruin back then, but not as much of a ruin as it is now.

"Tell me more about Mary Jones," you say after breakfast – a large cooked meal. Your Mum and Dad certainly enjoyed it.

"As you know, Mary's story really centres around the Bible," Mrs Maddox explains. "Mary lived in the time of a great religious revival. The Anglican Church was going through a bad time in many parts of Wales in the 1700s, and some clergymen felt God was calling them to get out and teach the people about the Bible. This breakaway group came to be known as Methodists, started by John Wesley."

"Did that cause trouble?" you ask.

Mrs Maddox sighs. "It certainly did. People were arrested and thrown into prison for preaching in a building that wasn't a licensed church. And then the law was changed. Although officially still part of the Anglican Church at that time, the Methodists quickly started building their own places of worship. The Methodists, along with other groups, set up the special schools I mentioned yesterday."

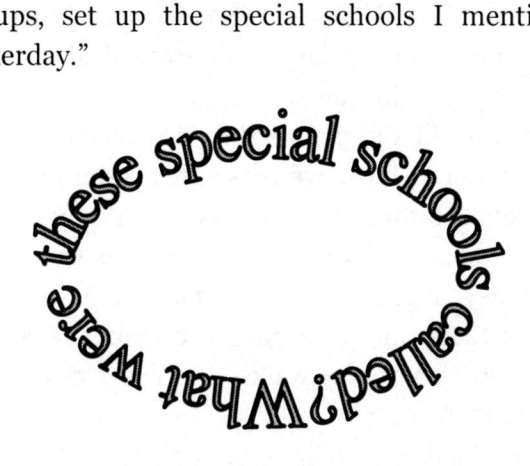

What were these special schools called?

HINT: They were to get people to think!

Mrs Maddox says, "They were called **Circulating Schools**, because they only stayed in each place for a few months, before moving on round to another village. After the teacher moved, someone from the village was usually chosen to keep things going. The main aim was to teach people to read and understand the Bible for themselves."

"I thought the people didn't have Bibles," you say, just to prove you were listening yesterday.

"People didn't generally have their *own* Bibles," Mrs Maddox explains, "but as soon as they could read, they might have been able to find a Welsh copy in their church or parish to look at. It's what Mary did, when she walked once a week to the farmhouse."

"And had to take her clogs off at the door," you say out loud. "So who exactly was Thomas Charles?" The name keeps popping up.

"The Rev'd Thomas Charles was an Anglican clergyman who came from south Wales. In 1783 he married a young woman from Bala. Her name was Sally Jones. She owned a shop in Bala, and didn't want to move south. So Thomas Charles moved to Bala and they lived above the shop. That was when he joined what were known as the Welsh Calvinistic Methodists, and decided to restart the schools."

You ask if Thomas Charles did all the teaching.

"He chose school teachers to do it, but he travelled around the area making sure everything was going well. Mary Jones was one of the brightest pupils in Abergynolwyn. She was so keen, that she quickly learnt parts of the Bible by heart. And of course her greatest wish, once she could read, was to have a Bible of her own and read it whenever she wanted."

Learning parts of the Bible off by heart may sound a bit strange to you. You wonder how many Bibles there are in your house. Two – three – four? Some of them may not have been opened for years. And here was a girl who had only just learnt to read, and the one thing she wanted in life was a Bible of her own!

"So Mary started saving," Mrs Maddox says. "A coin here, a coin there. Bibles were very expensive, and she thought she would never have enough. Then one day it seems she met the Rev'd Thomas Charles, who was travelling down here on his horse. A young person called Lizzie Rowlands used to listen to Mary's stories when Mary was very old. Many years later Lizzie Rowlands wrote down what she remembered Mary telling her about the walk to Bala." Mrs Maddox reaches for a folder containing copies of some of Lizzie Rowland's letters and talks, dated between 1885 and 1910. "Here is what Lizzie Rowlands says Mary told her."

One stormy Monday morning, as I was walking to a farmhouse about two miles from my home, a gentleman riding on a white horse and wearing a cloth cape came to meet me and asked me where I was going through such wind and rain.

I said I was going to a farmhouse where there was a Bible, that there wasn't one nearer my home, and that the mistress of the farm had said that I could see the Bible, which she kept on a table in the parlour, so long as I took my clogs off.

I told him that I was saving up every halfpenny this long time to get a Bible, but that I did not know where I could get one. The gentleman was 'Charles of Bala'. He told me to come to Bala at a certain time, that he was expecting some from London and that I should have one from him.

Thomas Charles of Bala

Mrs Maddox shows you a picture of Thomas Charles in an old book. Then she takes out a larger book, and says, "This is *The Sunday Schools of Wales* published in 1883."

She opens it at a page showing an engraving of a girl walking along in the countryside. The title under the picture says: *Mary Jones on her way – Cader Idris in the background.*

"Cadair Idris is the standard spelling now," Mrs Maddox explains, "although it's called Cader Idris on old maps and in old books. Look at the pictures carefully. If that's Cadair Idris, Mary Jones must be on her way home, because she should be walking the other way with the mountain in the background! Cadair Idris is to the north of here, and Mary walked east to Bala. But never mind, I've made nine copies of the original for you, but I did some changes with my computer to all of them except one. There are four matching pairs and one original. **Which is the original?**"

Turn the page for the puzzle.

Mary Jones and Her Bible

HINT

The original is one of these missing.

AN ADVENTURE BOOK CHRIS WRIGHT

Mary Jones and Her Bible

The answer is picture D. (Pairs are A and F; C and G; B and H; E and I.)

"While we were looking at Mary's cottage yesterday," Mrs Maddox says, "did you spot a mistake with her age on the memorial? It was erected in 1921, and they should have known better."

You tell Mrs Maddox that you read that Mary walked to Bala when she was sixteen, and you've no reason to doubt it.

"Mary was born just before Christmas in 1784," Mrs Maddox tells you. "Of that we can be sure. She travelled to Bala to buy the Bible in the spring or early summer of 1800. Of that, too, we can be sure. You're right, the memorial says she was sixteen." She turns to a page in Mary Ropes' old book, and shows you a copy of Mary's writing in her Bible. "How old does she say she was?"

"In her sixteenth year," you say.

"How old was Mary in her sixteenth year?"

You say sixteen.

"How old were you in your first year? Were you one?" Mrs Maddox asks.

You say of course not. You were less than one.

"So how old were you in your second year?"

You work out you were aged one, and not yet two, and slowly the light dawns.

"So how old was *Mary* in her second year?"

"She was one year old. So she must have been fifteen in her sixteenth year." And of course that is exactly what it says rather faintly in Mary's Bible:

"*I bought this in the 16th year of my age.*"

You ask why so many people could have got Mary's age wrong. **Why did they?**

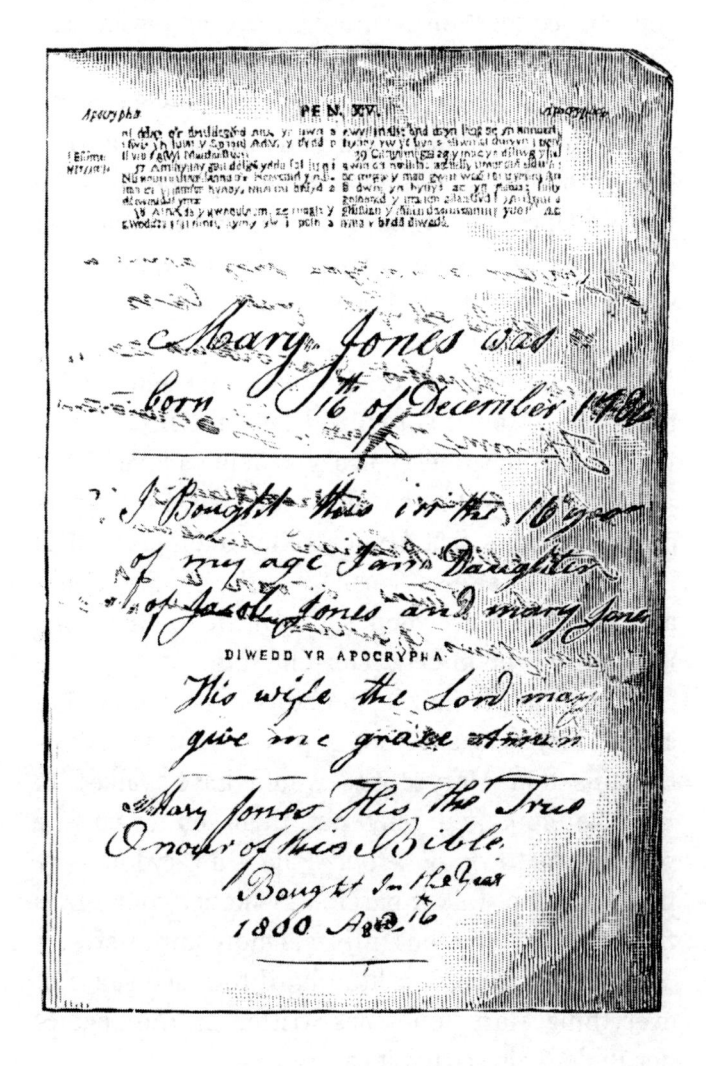

Mrs Maddox shrugs. "Perhaps someone read the inscription in the Bible quickly and didn't do the maths. If you examine the actual page in her Bible, you can see the ᵗʰ on 16 more clearly, and even here on this old engraving you can see that she ends with *Bought in the year 1800 aged 16ᵗʰ*. Maybe people didn't know in what month Mary Jones was born – that's more likely, and missed the importance of the 16ᵗʰ bit. Of course, whoever organised the memorial may never have seen Mary Jones's Bible, and took someone's word for it. Mary's Bible was given to the Bible Society in 1880."

"And no one bothered to work her age out for themselves, and it got copied onto the inscription. It's been set in stone," you say, making a joke of it.

Mrs Maddox laughs and seems to like your joke, or maybe she's just being polite. She agrees it is indeed set in stone. "I can't see there's any doubt about Mary's age when she walked to Bala. She *must* have been fifteen," she tells you.

You think it makes the story even better. Because Mary's clogs were very precious, Mrs Maddox explains that Mary Jones would have walked to Bala barefoot and only put them on when she reached the town. *Barefoot?* Bala is a very long way if you have to walk it barefoot, whether your age is fifteen or sixteen – but fifteen is more impressive.

You're finding it a little hard to make sense of everything Mary Jones has written on the page of her Bible. This is what it says:

An Adventure Book   Chris Wright

> *Mary Jones was*
> *Born 16th of December 1784*
>
> ———————
>
> *I Bought this in the 16th year*
> *of my age I am Daughter*
> *of Jacob Jones and mary Jones*
>
> *His wife the Lord may*
> *give me grace Amen*
>
> ———————
>
> *Mary Jones His The True*
> *Onour of this Bible*
> *Bought In the Year*
> *1800 Aged 16th*

There is no punctuation, there are two spelling mistakes, and some wrong or missing capital letters. You can look back a page to the engraving if it helps. **Use a piece of paper and write it out correctly.**

HINT: You will have to change some of the spelling, and change where sentences start and

The spelling mistakes are *onour (owner)* and *His (is)*. This is how it should have been written, with the correct spelling, capital letters and punctuation:

> *Mary Jones was*
> *born 16th of December 1784*
>
> *I bought this in the 16th year of my age. I am [the] daughter of Jacob Jones and Mary Jones his wife*
>
> *The Lord may give me grace, Amen*
>
> *Mary Jones is the true owner of this Bible, bought in the year 1800, aged 16th.*

Mrs Maddox says, "You have to remember that Mary Jones spoke Welsh, not English. So she did very well. English was the official language for filling out forms, so maybe Mary felt this inscription was so important that she should make it look like an official document. Or perhaps someone wrote it out for her in English, with the two spelling mistakes, and she copied it into her Bible exactly as it was written. If she didn't understand English, she wouldn't have known how to space it out, which is why some words are on the wrong lines."

Your Dad calls you, and you think he's telling you to change so you can hike into Bala, but what he's really saying is, **"Can you change HIKE into BALA, changing one letter at a time but always spelling a word?"**

> It is probably a good idea to copy the puzzle onto a sheet of paper, rather than write in this book.

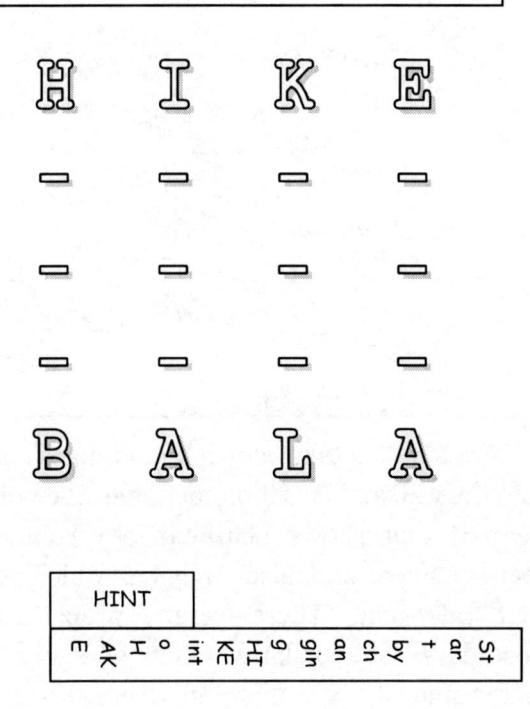

HIKE

☐ ☐ ☐ ☐

☐ ☐ ☐ ☐

☐ ☐ ☐ ☐

BALA

HINT

make Hi or int KE HI going an ch by t ar St

You write down HIKE, HAKE, BAKE, BALE, and BALA, or maybe you found another way to do it, like HIKE, BIKE, BILE, BALE, and BALA. So, you're off to Bala, the place to which Mary Jones walked to buy a Bible from Thomas Charles.

"We're going to try and follow the route Mary took," your Mum says.

"Did she walk on the roads?" you ask in surprise. "I was imagining her walking over the mountains."

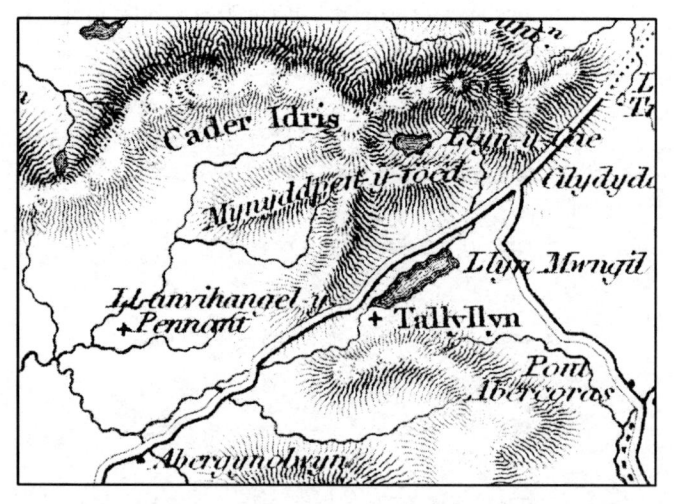

Mrs Maddox takes down an old map in a frame from the wall and lays it on the table. She points out the part that shows Llanfihangel-y-Pennant and Abergynolwyn, and also Tallyllyn which today is spelt Tal-y-llyn. "There weren't proper roads in those days," she explains. "And the squiggly lines on the map are streams and rivers. Roads as we know them came with motor cars. But of course there were tracks, wide enough for a horse and cart between towns and villages. But certainly nothing with a smooth surface."

You study the map. Mrs Maddox says it was drawn around 1835, so any roads would probably have been there when Mary did the walk in 1800.

"It's not shown here, but you can climb a steep mountain pass behind Mary's cottage," she says. "Once Mary Jones was over that, she would have dropped down to the road between Abergynolwyn and Tal-y-llyn. Then it's two very long valleys between here and Bala. That's not to say it was an easy walk for anybody, let alone a girl of fifteen walking barefoot."

Mrs Maddox goes on to say that Mary probably cut some corners using small tracks. "It would have saved her a mile or more if she did."

Bala is a town north-west of Llanfihangel-y-Pennant, on the edge of a large lake, but it's not on this part of the map.

Your Mum has already put a few things together for the journey – important things like food – and tells you to make sure you have some warm clothes. She thinks it's going to be chilly after all the rain of the past few days.

You can hear your Dad out at the car. He's checking something under the bonnet, which is just as well – because *you* don't intend to complete the journey on foot!

A few minutes later you're leaving Llanfihangel-y-Pennant and climbing the hilly road over to Abergynolwyn. You can't see him properly from the back seat, but you think your Dad really *is* keeping his eyes open as he drives over the ups and downs of the narrow road, with the steep drop to the right.

"We'll soon be on a wider road," Dad says cheerfully, as he slows down to miss an oncoming car in a small passing place marked with the Welsh words *Man Pasio*. "Help me find the shortest way from here to Bala on this old map."

Mrs Maddox has lent your Dad a photocopy of another antique map, so you can see how the old roads ran in Mary Jones's time. Mrs Maddox has marked Llanfihangel and Bala with an arrow.

Your Dad pulls into a lay-by and traces out the route with his finger on the map. Suddenly he laughs. "Let me ask you a riddle. Imagine you're driving a bus from Llanfihangel here, to Bala . . . there." He points to the two arrows. "At Llanfihangel the bus is empty, but ten passengers get on in Abergynolwyn. Another passenger gets on at Tal-y-llyn. No one gets off."

Dad keeps his finger tracing the route. "Near Dolgellau, which is spelt Dolgelley on this old map, three of the passengers get off and no one gets on."

You're busy counting with your fingers, and seem to be following it okay.

"At the next stop two passengers get off, and five get on. Next stop, four get on and no one gets off. At Llanuwchllyn, two passengers get off and no one gets on. At Bala everyone gets off."

You're feeling pretty confident with your numbers now.

"All right," Dad says, "what's the name of the bus driver?"

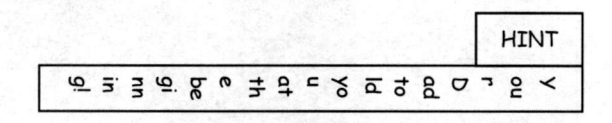

HINT
You're driving the bus, silly!

Mary Jones and Her Bible

Your Dad told you the answer when he asked the question – *you are driving the bus*!

Here are two old pictures Mrs Maddox gave you of Mary Jones on her way to Bala. The long bag over Mary's shoulder is called a wallet – not to be confused with a small wallet that goes in your pocket. In the wallet she will be carrying her clogs and her food. On the way back she will also use it to carry her Bible – if she gets one!

AN ADVENTURE BOOK   CHRIS WRIGHT

The two pictures are not identical. The first one is an exact copy of a picture in the 1882 book about Mary Jones by MER (Mary Ropes). Can you find five big changes Mrs Maddox has made with her computer in the picture below?

In the picture on the right: Mary's hat is taller, the tree on the top right has lost a branch, the far hills are missing in the top left, there is a white patch on Mary's apron, and there's an extra bush on the bottom left.

Soon you leave the village of Abergynolwyn and reach a long, narrow lake. "This is Tal-y-llyn Lake," your Dad says, "although it's not spelt on old maps as it is today. Like the name Cadair Idris, a lot of place names have now been changed back to the earlier Welsh, rather than using the spelling the English gave them."

Your Mum suddenly calls out that she's seen an otter in the lake, but no one else has. Anyway, your Dad seems too excited by the thought of tracking Mary's route to think of anything else.

"No one can say for certain which side of the lake Mary walked along," he tells you. "There would have been a track on either side, but this road is fairly modern. You can see where it's been cut into the rock. My guess is that Mary walked on the other side, as it would have been very marshy over here in 1800. But we'll soon join up with her route."

Your Mum is determined to be heard, and points to an old church by the side of the lake. "Saint Mary's Church," she says. "It's where Mary Jones married Thomas Jones in February 1813, when she was twenty-eight. She was living near Abergynolwyn at the time, and this was the nearest church that was registered to carry out weddings."

A mountain rises high above the church, and with the lake by its side it looks like a wonderful place in which to get married. But right now Mary is only fifteen, and she still has nearly twenty-five miles (40km) to walk before she gets to Bala!

Soon, your modern road links up with the track on the far side of the lake, and the village of Tal-y-llyn is left far behind,

There's a bit of a climb as you switch valleys in the car to the one in which Bala lies, but other than that the road is fairly level. Your parents stop to view the scenery from time to time, and it takes you well over an hour to get to Bala and park the car.

Your Mum says, "We're looking for the building where the Rev'd Thomas Charles lived with his wife Sally when they got married. **Can you remember what type of building it was?**"

| HINT | It belonged to his wife. Worked on her parents. |

Your Dad shows you MER's 1882 book on Mary Jones. It has an engraving of the **shop where Thomas Charles lived**. "It's still here," he says, "but it may take some finding."

You see lots of shops in the main street of Bala, and there are probably more in the side streets. "Give me a clue," you beg.

"Right," Dad says, "I think you can *bank* on getting it right in the end."

You find this building, which is certainly a bank, but it seems to be much wider than the one in the old picture. **Can it possibly be the same place?**

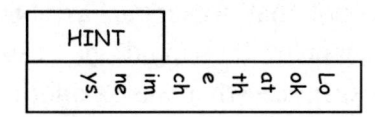

HINT

Look at the time on the keys.

The building *is* the same one, but the bank has taken over the building on the right, which is where Thomas Charles and his wife lived later.

Your Dad explains that all the fancy stonework above the windows, and on the roof, has been added later to make the building more impressive. And, of course, the old picture is a drawing, not a photograph, so not every detail will be accurate.

You stand back and your Dad tells you to read these plaques on the front wall, just in case you're still in doubt.

You know enough about Mary Jones now to spot that someone has got the year of her death wrong. It should be 1864, not 1866. You're surprised that wasn't another question, to see how observant you are!

"You'll remember that Mrs Maddox told us that Thomas Charles came from south Wales," Dad says, sounding knowledgeable. "This is the shop his wife was keeping when she married him. It turned out to be an excellent arrangement, because she was able to support her husband financially, which let him get on with his preaching and writing."

You say this sounds a bit cheeky, but your Mum explains that other preachers came to this arrangement. "Methodist preachers weren't paid a salary," she says, "and their wives were great supporters of what they were doing. So I don't think you need feel sorry for Sally Charles!"

"What sort of shop was it?" you ask.

Your Mum writes something down. "**Solve the puzzle,** she says, **then you'll know what sort of shop it was.**"

REHS ADR EBAH

HINT

Think about stuff or things making clothes.

You read it backwards and discover it was a **HABERDASHER**, which your Mum says is an old-fashioned name for a shop that sells thread, ribbons and buttons, and sometimes hats and gloves.

Mrs Maddox has lent your Dad photocopies of some pages from the large book called *Sunday at Home* for 1878. The introduction says, *"All the main facts in the following narrative were derived from two friends now departed, who were intimately acquainted with both the Rev'd Thomas Charles of Bala and the little Welsh Sunday scholar."* It goes on:

The "one thing" Mary's heart desired through all those long years was to possess a Bible of her own. Every penny she received from kind neighbours for any small services she deposited in her little treasury. [. . .] At last she could rejoice over the amount required. She was, however, informed that no copy of the Welsh Bible could be had nearer than Bala, of Mr Charles, and that it was doubtful whether he had a single copy. She was not, however, to be discouraged, and determined to go and inquire.

Upon a bright morning in the spring of 1800, the young girl rose with the dawn, and started off towards Bala in search of a Bible. She had had the loan of a wallet to carry the Divine treasure home safely, should Heaven and Mr Charles grant her anxious wishes. She had too a pair of rustic shoes to put on at her journey's end when she reached the house [. . .] It was late in the evening when Mary reached Bala – too late to see Mr Charles that night, as it was one of his rules when at home to be "early to bed, and early to rise."

As instructed before starting, Mary called upon a humble but much respected Methodist preacher at Bala, of the name of David Edwards. He questioned her. Mary's intelligent replies, and the affecting object of her journey, soon secured the venerable father's deepest interest in her success. "Well, my dear little girl, it is too late," he said, "to see Mr Charles to-night; he always retires to bed early, but he rises in the morning with the earliest dawn. Thou shalt sleep here to-night, and we will go to Mr Charles as soon as I see light in his study window to-morrow morning, so that thou mayest reach home before night."

The following morning her friend, David Edwards, aroused the young stranger at earliest dawn, and together they directed their steps towards Mr Charles's house. There was light in the study window. [. . .]

"It truly grieves me," he [Thomas Charles] remarked to his friend, "to see the little girl come all the distance from Llanfihangel here to buy a Bible, and I without a Bible to give her. The last supply of Welsh Bibles I received last year from London has been all sold out months ago, excepting a few copies I have kept for friends whom I must not disappoint. The society in London, which has for many years supplied Wales with Bibles, has now positively refused to print for us a single copy more. What I shall do for Welsh Bibles for my country again I know not." [. . .]

Despite his obligations to other friends, Mr Charles could not resist the appeal. "My dear child," he said, "I see you must have a Bible, difficult as it is for me to spare you one. It is impossible to refuse you." [. . .]

This visit made an indelible impression upon Mr Charles. Often did he bring the girl's history forward in his appeals to wealthy friends in England on behalf of Wales.

"Now," Dad says, "what exactly happened here in Bala that day? The earliest account we have is a short article in the *Bible Society Monthly Reporter* for January 1, 1867. It's yet another story that came from someone who knew someone who knew Mary Jones. In that account Mary is also given one Bible. But in a manuscript in the National Library of Wales, Mary is given an extra one for her aunt, and in Lizzie Rowland's account she is given three. Here is what Lizzie Rowlands says Mary Jones told her nearly sixty years after the walk to Bala, and Lizzie Rowlands wrote it down a lot later in letters and talks between 1885 and 1907."

"I came to Bala, and trembling, knocked on the door of Mr Charles's house. I asked for Mr Charles. He was in his study which was at the back of the house. I was allowed to go to him, and he told me that the Bibles had not arrived. I started to cry because I did not know where to stay. He sent me to stay with an old servant of his who had a house at the bottom of his garden, until the Bibles came. When they came, Mr Charles gave me *three* for the money, that is for the price of one. I set off home with my precious burden. I ran a great part of the way, I was so glad of my Bible."

Surely Mary couldn't have *run* home with three heavy Bibles in her wallet. You note that she says she was so glad of her *Bible*, not *Bibles.* And where were the Bibles coming from that Lizzie Rowlands said Mary had to wait for? She doesn't tell us, but probably from London. Of course, it's possible that Mary was only sent to stay with the old servant for a couple of hours while someone fetched a Bible or Bibles from a store somewhere in Bala. Lizzie Rowlands says Mary was given three copies; a manuscript in the National Library of Wales says two; the *Bible Society Monthly Reporter* for January 1 1867 says she was given one; *Sunday at Home* for 1878 also says she was given one; and in 1882 Mary Ropes (MER) wrote that Mary Jones had a single Bible from a cupboard in Thomas Charles' study. One, two or three? It's certainly a puzzle!

Your Dad smiles. "Right," he says suddenly, "let's see how good *you* are at remembering things. **What year was it when Mary walked here to Bala to see Thomas Charles?**"

Mary Jones and Her Bible

It was 1800.

There's a small market in the town. Apart from the usual clothing stalls and people selling hardware, you find a table set out with old books. Three of the books are very old Welsh Bibles. You feel a bit like Mary Jones coming here to buy one in 1800!

The covers are coming off all of them, and many of the pages are torn and creased. It looks as though children have been using some of the pages to practise their writing and drawing skills in the past. Even so, you turn the pages carefully, while the woman keeping the stall watches you warily. Yes, you know that old books must be handled gently, even when they're falling apart like these.

"Old Bibles," the woman says, in a strong Welsh accent. "Are you looking for anything in particular?"

You explain about your interest in Mary Jones. Of course, you're not expecting to find *her* Bible, but one of these might be just like it. Unfortunately, you have no idea how big hers was. There's a very large Bible, a large one and a medium sized one. The large Bible is surprisingly thick.

The woman says she doesn't know what Mary Jones's Bible looked like. As far as she's concerned, these are just old Bibles. You ask how much they are.

She shrugs and says they're in very poor condition – which is obvious. Then she mentions a price that is just within your reach. You feel excited. After all, where are you going to find an old Welsh Bible again – especially one you can afford?

There are dates in the front of each Bible, in Roman numerals – and you're not too good on those. Then you remember Mrs Maddox saying that the Welsh Bibles that Thomas Charles sold were printed in Oxford in 1799. Unfortunately, none of these has the word Oxford in the front, but deep down you have a feeling that one of these is *exactly* like Mary's. So what are you to do?

This is what you read. The first one is a large family Bible. It says, MDCCXCVII and was printed in somewhere called Caerfyrddin. The middle size one says, MDCCXCIX and was printed in Rhydychen, and the smallest Bible is still quite large. It says MDCCCXLVI, printed in Caer Grawnt.

If only Mrs Maddox was here, she'd know for sure. A man is looking over your shoulder, and he also seems interested in the Bibles. If you're going to buy one, you'll have to make up your mind *very* quickly. And you can't afford all three! This is what they look like. The pencil gives an idea of the size of each one. The largest is shown first, and the smallest last.

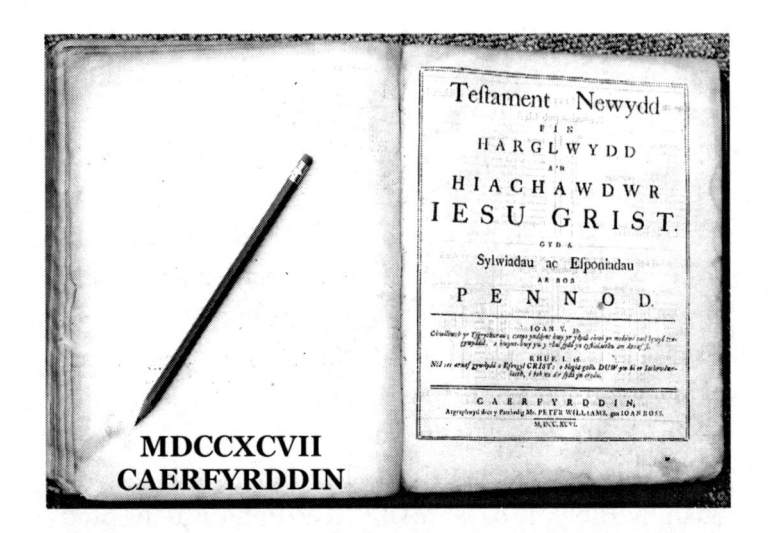

Testament Newydd
EIN
HARGLWYDD
A'N
HIACHAWDWR
IESU GRIST.
GYDA
Sylwiadau ac Esponiadau
AR BOB
PENNOD.

MDCCXCVII
CAERFYRDDIN

Testament Newydd
EIN
HARGLWYDD
A'N
HIACHAWDWR
IESU GRIST.

MDCCXCIX
RHYDYCHEN

An Adventure Book — Chris Wright

"I'll have one," you say, pulling the money from your pocket. The thought of missing out on a Bible that might be exactly like Mary's is too terrible to think about.

The three Bibles are open at the start of the New Testament. Be quick! Which one do you choose?

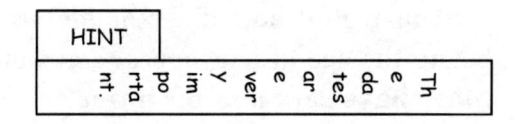

HINT: The dates are very important.

You should have chosen the middle Bible printed in MDCCXCIX in Rhydychen, and you'll learn why when you get back to Mrs Maddox in *Ty'n-y-mynydd*.

You Mum and Dad have finished their coffee and they join you. You show them the Bible. Dad is impressed, but you have a feeling your Mum isn't too keen on the ancient leather cover that's already shedding bits of brown all over your clothes.

There's a statue of Thomas Charles in the town. You compare it with the 1882 picture in your Dad's old book by Mary Ropes, and it looks much the same – although the artist seems to have put remarkably small people in the foreground. Even so, it's impressive, and an indication of the high regard in which the Rev'd Thomas Charles was, and still is, held by the people of Bala.

The journey back should be quick. Of course, you have to remember that Mary walked it both ways. Your Mum wonders how Mary's mother felt about it. Mary was supposed to be back the next day, but maybe she had to stay in Bala for a few days if the Bibles were still on their way from London.

You realise how different life was then, long before the age of telephones. You wonder. **Could Mary have sent a letter home?**

Thomas Charles

Yes she could, but this was before the days of the national postage rate of one penny in 1840, and a letter to Llanfihangel-y-Pennant in 1800 by coach would have been expensive and would probably have taken several days to arrive, by which time Mary would have been home.

Your Mum says she's sure Mary's mother would have worried that she was lost or injured somewhere along the way. Yes, life has certainly changed. And to think you were bothered that you couldn't get a signal for your phone in Llanfihangel-y-Pennant!

Your Mum is driving back, and she unexpectedly stops by a country church not far out of Bala, on the edge of the lake, and tells you to get out.

Well, bits are still falling off the cover of your old Bible, but it only smells a bit of damp, and you can't think of anything you've done wrong.

She laughs when she sees your expression in the driving mirror. "I'm only joking," she says, passing you a paper napkin. "We're all getting out in a minute. First, pretend this is your map home. I scribbled it out when Dad and I were having coffee. Start at the top in Bala. Don't follow it with you finger. Just use your eyes. Then we'll go and find the grave of Thomas Charles in the churchyard here in Llanycil.

Can you get back to Llanfihangel-y-Pennant from Bala without making a single mistake?

AN ADVENTURE BOOK   CHRIS WRIGHT

Llanycil Church and Bala Lake in 1880

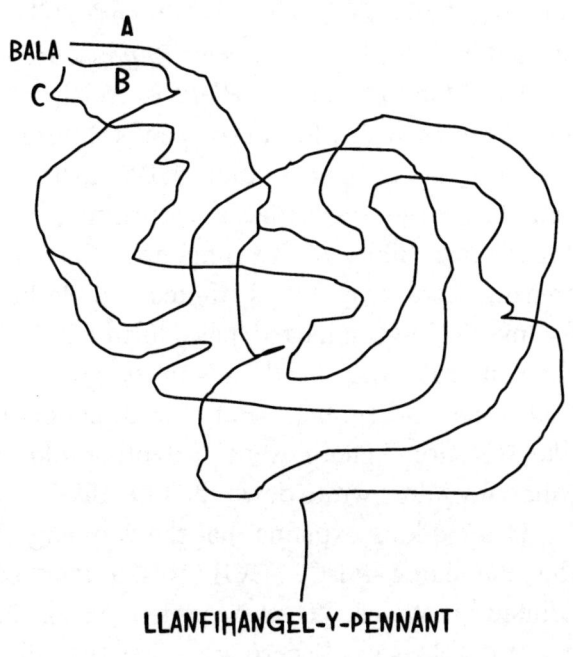

BALA
    A
  C B

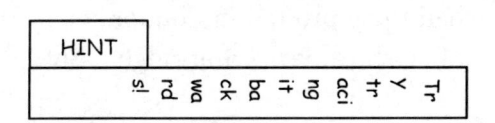

LLANFIHANGEL-Y-PENNANT

HINT sl rd wa ck ba it ng aci tr y Tr

101

The answer is route C.

Mrs Maddox welcomes you back for tea. The first thing she sees is your old Bible. "Why," she exclaims, "that's *just* like Mary Jones's Bible!"

You are about to lay it on the table, but your Mum is still fussing about the bits of old leather dropping everywhere. You don't really care if it's falling to pieces, because it seems that you chose the right one after all.

Mrs Maddox puts a newspaper on the table and you place the Bible on it. "I wasn't sure about it," you say. "You told me Mary Jones's Bible was printed in Oxford. This one says *Rhydychen*."

Mrs Maddox laughs. "*Rhyd* is Welsh for ford, and *Ychen* is Welsh for an ox. That's Oxford. Don't you worry about the condition. MDCCXCIX. This is definitely from the same 1799 printing as Mary Jones's own Bible. You've come up with something amazing here. I've always wanted a Bible like this for myself. Did you have to pay a fortune?"

You shake your head. "It's in too poor a condition to be worth much." But to you, of course, it's like treasure. "There were two other old Welsh Bibles for sale. I wrote down their details."

Mrs Maddox explains that the very large Bible, the one dated MDCCXCVII, was a 1797 edition printed in Wales. "There's something fascinating about it," she says. "There was a law that all Bibles had to be printed in London, or by the Universities of Oxford or Cambridge. But Peter Williams realised that if he included a commentary on the verses in his translation, he could print it anywhere, because technically it was no longer a Bible. He published it first in 1770 in Caerfyrddin, the Welsh name for Carmarthen. Thomas Charles, among others, wasn't too happy with parts of the commentary, which is why he bought the 1799 Bible that was printed at a bargain price in Oxford for the SPCK, without any notes."

"What about the third, smaller Bible?" you ask. "It was dated MDCCCXLVI, and printed in Caer Grawnt."

"*Caer Grawnt* is the Welsh name for Cambridge," Mrs Maddox explains. "MDCCCXLVI? You should have known it couldn't be anything to do with Mary Jones!"

Why does Mrs Maddox say this?

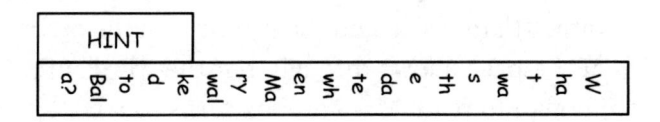

HINT
Was that a Bible to do with Mary Jones?

MDCCCXLVI is the date **1846** in Roman numerals, and **Mary walked to Bala in 1800**! You measure up the Bible you've bought – the one just like Mary's – and it's 8½ by 5½ inches, and a little over 3 inches thick. That's about 21 by 15 by 8 centimetres. And it weighs well over three pounds (about 1.5kg). As you thought in Bala, two or three Bibles would have weighed Mary down on her walk home – if she really came back with more than one.

It's raining again now, and much too wet to venture out. "I'm going to show you my favourite Bible verse, in Welsh," Mrs Maddox says after tea. "We'll look it up in the Bible you've just bought. Mary's own Bible, of course, is safely in the University Library of Cambridge."

You feel quite excited to be reading the same words placed exactly as Mary Jones saw them in her own Bible from Bala. The letters are brown rather than black, and the printing on the other side of the page shows through, but the words are clear enough to read. Mrs Maddox turns to a book in the Bible called *Ioan* in Welsh, and in one of the chapters finds a verse with the number 16.

> 16 ¶ ⁿ Canys, felly y carodd Duw y byd, fel y rhoddodd efe ei unig-anedig Fab, fel na choller pwy bynnag a gredo ynddo ef, ond caffael o hono fywyd tragywyddol.

"Now," she says, "here's the same verse in the Good News Bible, which is published by Bible Society.

"For God loved the world so much that he gave his only Son, so that everyone who believes in him may not die but have eternal life."

Mrs Maddox is keeping her Bible hidden, so you can't see where she's reading from, but it's a verse you've heard before.

She looks up at you. **"You know the verse is 16. But can you give me the name of the book and the chapter in the Bible these words come from?"**

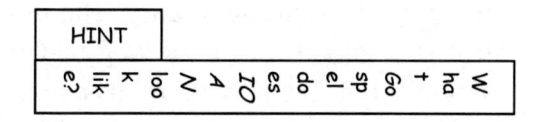

HINT

Was that a good episode of204 Kilroy?

The book called Ioan in the Welsh Bible is the **Gospel of John**, and the **chapter is 3.** Maybe you remember it now: **John 3:16.**

"Are you *sure* Mary Jones's Bible is in the University Library of Cambridge?" you ask, wondering if there's *any* chance hers is the one you've just bought in Bala.

"Absolutely sure," Mrs Maddox says, closing your Welsh Bible.

Well, that's the end of that exciting possibility. "Have you seen it?" you ask.

Mrs Maddox smiles and nods. "You have to arrange it through the Library. The Bible was once open in a glass case for so long that in the end it wouldn't shut. It's now been taken apart section by section, and repaired and rebound. But it's definitely the right one. It has Mary Jones's writing on some of the pages, just as I showed you yesterday."

You remember that now, and could kick yourself for even wondering if you'd bought Mary Jones's own Bible!

"There was at least one other," Mrs Maddox goes on, which makes your heart skip a beat. Then she adds, "It's safely in the National Library of Wales in Aberystwyth."

So that's another possibility out of the window.

"The story goes that Mary brought one back for her aunt, but some people believe that Mary brought back three."

"Dad told me about that in Bala," you say, as you pick up your copy and try to imagine carrying three of these on foot for twenty-six miles. "Why doesn't anyone know for sure?"

Mrs Maddox sighs. "The earliest account of Mary's walk to Bala was written in 1867, which was nearly seventy years afterwards. There are several written accounts, but not all the details can be right. The problem is, no one seems to have made any records at the time, and everyone in the Bala story was dead by the time people started writing the story of Mary Jones. Even Lizzie Rowlands waited years before putting pen to paper. The only person who seems to have written anything at the time is Mary Jones herself – in her Bible. *Bought in the year 1800 Aged 16th.*"

So that's why no one can confirm the fine details. Things were all second-hand by the time of the first formal account was written sixty-seven years after the walk to Bala. You tell Mrs Maddox that you're completely confused.

Your Mum has been listening with great interest. **"How many Bibles do *you* think Mary brought back?"** she asks you.

You look to Mrs Maddox for help, but she just laughs. "Answer your mother's question," she says!

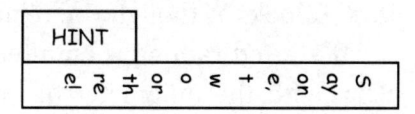

HINT
Say two, or three!

You mutter to yourself a bit, and say nothing sensible.

"The answer is that **no one knows**," Mrs Maddox says, putting you out of your misery. "So it doesn't matter what number you come up with! Well, yes, somebody somewhere may know," she adds. "How would you like to turn detective?"

This sounds fun, and Mrs Maddox gets out several old books. Some of them are books that your Dad has already shown you copies from. There's the large *Sunday at Home* volume dated 1878, Mary Ropes' book first published in 1882 with the long title *From the Beginning or The Story of Mary Jones and Her Bible*, and copies of various magazines. There's a book in the Welsh language called *Mary Jones* by Robert Oliver Rees dated 1879. Mrs Maddox says Robert Oliver Rees got his account from Mary's pastor in Bryn-crug, when Mary was very old.

There are other old books with paper markers in between some pages. You can see *The Sunday Schools of Wales* dated 1883 with a few pages about Mary, including the picture of her on the way to Bala – or perhaps on her way back, as Mrs Maddox said! And there's another Welsh book, *Y Tadau Methodistaidd* dated 1897, with yet more engravings. It looks as though you're in for a busy evening!

It started raining soon after you got back from Bala, with the milometer on the car showing just over fifty-two miles, which is over eighty kilometres. The rain has stopped now, and Mrs Maddox suggests a walk to Llanfihangel Church, which sounds like an excellent idea. You enjoy reading, but these books could be hard going – and you need some fresh air to help you keep awake.

"There's a building in the woods that will come as a big surprise," Mrs Maddox tells you. "Let's go and look for it now while it's still light, unless you're too tired."

You feel weary enough to drop after the excitement of Bala and buying the Welsh Bible, but you want to see what's in the woods.

"It's the farmhouse where Mary Jones went with her mother when she was young." Mrs Maddox explains. She writes something down. **"Can you remember the name?"**

> YES, LET'S LOOK EVERYWHERE CAREFULLY, HOWEVER WEARILY EVERYONE DROPS DOWN.

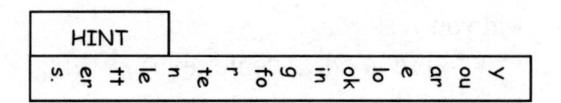

HINT

y pob gair cyntaf tua'r letre's

You take the first letter of each word and come up with *Y Llechwedd*, which Mrs Maddox says means *The Hillside*.

Your Mum and Dad say they'll be staying in *Ty'n-y-mynydd* by the fire, but you want to get out and explore before starting all that reading and thinking. Maybe you *will* turn detective some day, and work out for sure what happened in Bala, as well as solving all the other puzzles about Mary Jones and her Bible.

Mrs Maddox suggests you wear old shoes and clothes, as the path will be very muddy. There's a small car park opposite the church, and Mrs Maddox leads you through it, and up a wide track leading to a house.

"Keep going," Mrs Maddox says. "This isn't it."

You go through a metal gate and there on the right you see the remains of a large, derelict stone building.

"This is *Y Llechwedd*, the house that belonged to William Hugh."

"Or Pugh," you say, recalling what Mrs Maddox told you yesterday.

"You're good at remembering things," she says with a wink.

You nod. "I'm doing my best," you tell her. "I never know what questions I'm going to be asked!"

The wreck of the farmhouse stands like a ghostly shape in the middle of the woods, with a stream running right past it. It's all rather romantic

– as long as you don't have to live here!

"This is where Mary came to the Methodist meetings," Mrs Maddox explains as you pull your foot out of a muddy patch. "She walked here with her mother."

"Carrying the lantern when it was dark," you add. Yes, you're remembering quite a lot of what you've been told about Mary Jones.

"There were Sunday services, and midweek ones," Mrs Maddox tells you. "It was unusual for someone as young as Mary to go to the midweek services, but I've read that she was allowed to go because she had to carry the lamp for her mother." She laughs. "I think there must be more to it than that. I've often wondered if Mary shared her simple faith with the older members, and so was always welcome – lamp or no lamp."

"You told me about the trouble with the Anglican Church," you say, "but didn't the Methodists have their own chapel somewhere around?"

"There wasn't an official Methodist chapel anywhere near here until 1806, and that was in Cwrt, just as you enter Abergynolwyn. Records show that the Cwrt chapel was a very poor building, with an earth floor and no pews. How would you fancy that on a Sunday?"

"Not a lot. So the Methodists could hold services wherever they wanted?" you ask. "Even in a farmhouse?"

Mrs Maddox sighs. "Things are different now, but in those days the authorities had some very strict rules. They persecuted William Hugh for holding services here. Things got so bad that all the local Methodists were afraid of being imprisoned. When Mary was born, the troubles were at their height. Later, everyone could worship in peace – in a farmhouse or in a chapel. But this was no ordinary farmhouse, as you're about to discover."

There's a grubby window in the wall of the house, and you creep forward to look through it to see what the place is like inside.

Mrs Maddox calls you back and you wonder if you're doing something wrong. Surely, with the old farmhouse such a wreck, there's not going to be anybody still living in there. Is there?

"Don't look so worried," she says, smiling. "I only want to ask you a question before you look through the window."

You wait for the question.

"Tell me what you think you're going to see inside," she says. "And no peeping first!"

You say you have no idea, so you find a dry patch to stand on and cup your hands around your eyes to see into the gloom. You almost jump back in surprise. **You can see a pulpit and wooden pews!**

"*It's a chapel!*" you call out in surprise. "That's amazing!"

What's not so amazing is the state the place is in. Not only is everything damp and mouldy from the leaking roof, but things have been thrown here and there.

"It's all so sad," you say slowly, still looking through the window.

"These things happen," Mrs Maddox says. "I suppose we should be grateful there is anything left at all for us to see. It's possible that this chapel was built onto the farmhouse after Mary and her mother came here, and they worshipped in the farmhouse, but this is definitely *Y Llechwedd*. Can you imagine Mary finding her way through these woods in the dark with her mother?"

To be honest you can't. It's easier to imagine Mary Jones as a young girl running around outside her cottage in daylight. But, yes, *Y Llechwedd* is certainly worth seeing. Mary's cottage and this farmhouse are derelict, but the old church can't have changed much. So one out of three buildings still useable isn't too bad. Not when you think about it like that.

Although the rain has stopped, large drops of

water keep dripping off the trees onto your head.

You shiver. "Is Mary Jones buried here?" you ask, looking warily at the large mounds of green moss growing all around. They might be graves.

Mrs Maddox smiles. "Bless you, no. Mary is buried in Bryn-crug. I'll be going there tomorrow. A grand grave it is. Mary's parents are buried in the churchyard here in Llanfihangel-y-Pennant."

You're not sure why, but you hurry on ahead, back down the path to the old church of Saint Michael. The low sun is shining again, and the churchyard seems unexpectedly welcoming after the damp and gloomy woods.

Mary's parents' gravestone is inside the circle

"Mary's mother was eighty when she died. How old was Mary's father when he died?" Mrs Maddox asks.

Mrs Maddox told you yesterday that **he was only thirty**.

Mrs Maddox says, "That's their grave, the one with the small slate headstone."

You go closer, and bend down to read the words on it.

HERE lieth the Body of Jacob Jones who died April 16th 1789 Aged 30. Also the Remains of Mary his wife who died March 4th 1837 Aged 80 years.

It gives you quite a shock to realise that Mary's parents are here, and that Mary's mother was a widow for nearly fifty years. Every time you discover something like this, the story of Mary's life becomes more and more real. And to think that Jacob died so young. It must have been a terrible ordeal both for Mary and her mother. No wonder things were hard with the main wage earner no longer around.

"You look a bit pale," Mrs Maddox says, staring at you closely.

You've been having a strange time. First, the old farmhouse in the woods with the dripping trees, and now a grave for people you almost seem to know.

"I have to get back to *Ty'n-y-mynydd*. You and your parents will be wanting your evening meal soon," Mrs Maddox says.

You're feeling hungry, and you also want to look further at the old books. So you decide to go with her – and not for any other reason, of course!

But Mrs Maddox stops. "Before we go back, I want to see what you think about a real-life puzzle. Look, the gravestone says that Jacob Jones died on April 16th 1789, but the church register says he was buried on March 21st 1789. That's over three weeks before he died. How can that be?"

It's a question she wants you to answer before going any further!

Indeed, how can it be? Nobody is buried before they die! You give up, shrug your shoulders, and ask Mrs Maddox what the answer is.

She laughs. "There are plenty of mysteries for you to solve if you turn detective. Perhaps someone got the date wrong on the gravestone. It's so nicely engraved that it might have been a shame to do another one."

"Do you believe that?" you ask.

Mrs Maddox shakes her head. "Not really. I think that the person entering the burial in the church register looked at the date of the burial before, which in the register is the ninth of March and, after writing twenty-one, copied the word March by mistake instead of putting April. The twenty-first of April would make five days between Jacob's death and his burial, which is about right."

Yes, that sounds likely. Even so, there seem to be lots on unanswered questions while tracing the details of the history of Mary Jones.

Mrs Maddox sees you frowning. "Don't let these little problems worry you," she says. "Most of what we know about Mary Jones is proven fact. She lived just down the lane in *Ty'n-y-ddôl* with her parents. Her father died when she was four. She went regularly with her mother to the old farmhouse called *Y Llechwedd*, and she wanted a Bible of her own. She walked well over a mile, or maybe two, to a farmhouse to read the Bible every week, and saved up for a few years to get one of her own."

You nod. That's somewhere between two and three kilometres. "And she walked to Bala to get one for herself, when she was fifteen," you say. "Well, one or two or three Bibles!" You smile, as suddenly all the problems fade into the background. The main part of the story is true, and surely people are allowed to have different memories on some of the details. It always happens with history. But one day you're going to try to solve *everything*!

Mrs Maddox seems to be reading your thoughts. "You can study all the old books and records," she says, "but you have to bear in mind that people weren't too strict about accuracy in those days. They tended to write things without checking the facts. If someone told them something, they wrote it down if it sounded interesting. Lizzie Rowlands was only young, and Mary Jones was in her late seventies when they spoke, and Mary's memory may not have been too reliable by then. So we have the memories of what Lizzie Rowlands was told a long time before, by Mary Jones trying to remember her own distant past. There was a gap of between eighty-five and a hundred and seven years between Mary's journey to Bala, and Lizzie Rowlands writing Mary's story down.

So, you ask, does that mean that Lizzie Rowlands was unreliable?

Mrs Maddox says we can't know for sure. Some parts of Lizzie Rowland's stories differ from the other written accounts. It's unfortunate she didn't write things down while she was visiting Mary Jones, but waited until many years later. However, the main details agree.

Your Mum and Dad are going to the shops in Barmouth tomorrow. "Your parents say you can stay back with me," Mrs Maddox says. "I have to go to Bryn-crug where Mary Jones lived when she was older. If you come with me, I'll show you her house, and on the way we'll stop off in Abergynolwyn so you can see the old Calvinistic Methodist chapel where Mary is buried."

You note that Mrs Maddox pronounces Bryn-crug as *Brinn-creeg*, which is all part of the tricky Welsh language, although to the Welsh it's probably *your* language that's the tricky one!

"So it's not the end of Mary Jones's story yet," you say, pleased that there are still things to discover.

"What you've seen is only the start," Mrs Maddox says. "Mary Jones's story is still going on today."

You're about to ask if she means that Mary Jones is still alive, which would be an extremely silly question, especially as she's buried in Bryn-crug. "Tell me more about it," you say.

"Meeting Mary Jones in 1800 made a big impression on the Rev'd Thomas Charles," Mrs

Maddox tells you. "Of course, Mary was not the only young person to walk a long distance to Bala to buy a Welsh Bible from him. He sold three thousand copies, but he would often tell the story of Mary Jones with great fondness, and go out of his way to meet the young weaver, as he called her, when he was in this area. In December 1802, two and half years after meeting Mary in Bala, Thomas Charles was addressing a meeting in London talking about the problem of getting Welsh Bibles cheaply enough for everyone to buy.

"'We could supply our own Bibles,' he said. This went down well, and at that moment everyone realised that if they could get a Bible printed in the Welsh language, they could get them printed in other languages and distribute them all over the world. So in 1804 Thomas Charles, with others, founded an organisation to do that."

"I read something about it on Thomas Charles's house in Bala," you say, remembering the plaque on the wall of the bank.

"The name of the society has six words," Mrs Maddox says. "I'll write them down here, but I'll jumble them up. Can you sort them out?"

British Society And The Foreign Bible

HINT

"It was **The British and Foreign Bible Society**," Mrs Maddox says, "but it's just called Bible Society now. They help people read and understand the Bible in their own language. As you might expect, there's a link on their website to their Welsh language pages."

Medallion issued by the British and Foreign Bible Society in 1821. The inscription says:
THE BRITISH AND FOREIGN BIBLE SOCIETY INSTITUTED 7TH MARCH 1804 FOR THE CIRCULATION OF THE HOLY SCRIPTURES WITHOUT NOTE OR COMMENT IN EVERY LANGUAGE OF THE WORLD.

Medallion showing Thomas Charles, issued in 1885 to celebrate "100 YEARS OF THE SUNDAY SCHOOL IN WALES."

A STATEMENT FROM BIBLE SOCIETY

We are passionate about ending Bible poverty – and working for a day when the Bible's God-given revelation, inspiration and wisdom is shaping the lives and communities of people everywhere.

Our last task is urgent because of what people, communities and even nations lose by not coming to embrace the Bible's life-changing message.

Our task is also huge because —

- More than 4,400 languages still wait for even one book of the Bible.
- Though a billion people can't read, only three per cent of languages have the Bible in audio.
- Every 5 seconds someone goes blind but the Bible in Braille exists in only 30 languages.
- A billion people live on less than 60p a day – making the Bible a luxury they can't afford.
- In our own land, the Bible is no longer a point of reference for everyday life.

That's why we are working to make the Bible available in the most relevant form. It's also why we are finding new and innovative ways of allowing the Bible to connect with the fabric of everyday life. And why we are working with the church to help it live out God's story in its daily life.

Continued on next page

THE CHALLENGE

Our task is to make sure the Bible's message is known, loved and understood everywhere. But that's not easy.

Although in some parts of the world the Bible plays a central role, in many others it is ignored or seen as irrelevant. And in too many areas its message has still hardly been heard at all, or has virtually disappeared from the day-to-day reality of people's lives.

All this means that our work has to be done with more energy, creativity and innovation than, perhaps, ever before. We are still, as ever, totally committed to making the Bible and Scriptures available where there are none, but to this core task we have added new activities. We are also working in the culture in four key areas of society — arts, media, education and politics — that carry great influence.

Continued on next page

AN ADVENTURE BOOK CHRIS WRIGHT

> **UNITED BIBLE SOCIETIES**
>
> In our fight to end Bible poverty, we are working in partnership with 145 national Bible Societies. We do so as part of a worldwide fellowship called the UNITED BIBLE SOCIETIES with a central support function that improves our effectiveness and increases our efficiency.
>
> Vital too are our partnerships with other mission organisations around the world. And our partnership with our supporters — individuals and churches — whose sacrificial giving, prayer and sheer hard work makes what we do possible.
>
> Bible Society, a Christian charity, exists to end Bible poverty. Bible poverty is robbing millions of the truth that Jesus can set them free. Your support will help create a world where the Bible's life-changing message shapes the lives of people everywhere.
>
> http://www.biblesociety.org/

Mrs Maddox asks you how many different languages you think the Bible has been translated into.

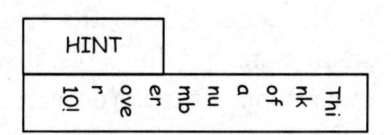

> HINT
> Think of a number of over 10!

Mrs Maddox says that, right now, the Bible is available in partial form in over 2,000 of the world's 6,900 known languages, the complete Bible in 429, and the New Testament in 1,144.

The next morning, as you're leaving on the way to Bryn-crug with Mrs Maddox by car, you ask her what happened to Mary Jones when she grew up.

"Mary Jones married Thomas Jones in 1813, in Saint Mary's Church by the side of Tal-y-llyn Lake."

You remember your Mum pointing out the church on the way to Bala, and telling you it was the nearest church to Abergynolwyn for marriages.

"Mary's husband was a weaver too," she tells you on the way over the winding road. Fortunately, Mrs Maddox seems to be keeping her eyes open. "Thomas and Mary lived just this side of Abergynolwyn, in Cwrt. There was the little Calvinistic Methodist chapel there by that time. We'll stop off so you can see it. It's not one of the large chapels in Abergynolwyn. They were built much later. The old chapel has been turned into two houses now, but you can still see it through the trees from the little car park by the Dysynni River."

A few minutes later Mrs Maddox parks the car and gets out. "Come on," she says, "or you'll miss it."

You look through the trees at a white building on the other side of the river, partly hidden by a small stone building. Yes, it was definitely a chapel once upon a time. You can see the outline of the long chapel windows that have now been filled in across the middle to make two floors.

Mrs Maddox is writing something down. "What type of chapel was it?" she asks, giving you a piece of paper.

Calm Division Itch Test

HINT

Two words of writing with it standing for a Methodist W.

Mrs Maddox has already told you that it was a **Calvinistic Methodist** chapel, and she now adds that the Calvinistic Methodist Church of Wales adopted a second name, the Presbyterian Church of Wales, which is what we usually call it now.

"Tell me about Mary when she married," you say, as you get back to the car.

Mrs Maddox seems pleased to be talking about Mary Jones, which means you're not driving her mad with your questions. She leaves the car engine switched off. "Mary's husband Thomas Jones was called Thomas Lewis, because his father's first name was Lewis."

"That doesn't make sense," you say.

"It's how things were done in those days. Call the child after the father's name."

"So Mary was called Mary Jacob locally, not Mary Jones," you say, laughing.

But Mrs Maddox takes it seriously. "Indeed she was. There, that's surprised you, hasn't it?"

It certainly has. You only meant it as a joke.

"Mary and her husband Thomas both worked as weavers. They lived here in Cwrt, and were regular chapel members. Thomas was one of the chapel elders."

"So did they live happily ever after?" you ask.

"Not by our standards today," Mrs Maddox tells you. "You have to remember that life was very hard, without modern health care and not enough money for food. They had at least six children. Some died when very young, and others lived into their teens, but maybe only one lived long enough to become an adult."

"That's terrible," you gasp.

"That's the way life was back then. Of course Mary and Jacob must have grieved for their loss, but they had a strong Christian faith that saw them through."

"So did Mary have anything to do with the British and Foreign Bible Society in later life?" you ask.

"She certainly did. She gave them money regularly."

"I thought she didn't have any money," you object.

"Nor did she," Mrs Maddox says.

"Then how . . . ?"

"I'm not saying she gave a lot, but she gave all she could, even though it meant living in poverty. When we get to Bryn-crug, I'll tell you what Lizzie Rowlands wrote when she visited Mary. But here is how Mary raised money for missionaries." Mrs Maddox writes something down. It's a Bible riddle from Judges 14:14. "It will be something to solve on the way," she says.

> *"Out of the eater came something to eat, out of the strong came something sweet."* Three days later they had still not solved the riddle.

The answer to the riddle is **honey.**

Hopefully it hasn't taken you three days to come up with the answer! Samson had seen bees nesting in the dead body of a lion, and he ate some of the honey.

"Mary kept bees," Mrs Maddox says. "She would let the bees crawl all over her, and they wouldn't sting."

You agree that there must have been something very special about Mary Jones. Giving away so much for missionary work that it meant living in poverty, showed just how much she loved God. And it seems that even the bees respected her!

You say, "It reminds me of what Jesus said when he saw a widow putting two mites into the temple treasury in Jerusalem."

"You're right," Mrs Maddox says. "Mites were the smallest coins you could get, but Jesus said the woman was giving more than anyone, because she was giving all she had. Everyone else was keeping plenty of their own money back."

You realise it was happening two thousand years ago in Jerusalem, and about two hundred years ago in Bryn-crug when Mary lived there. You wonder if it's still happening today. You hope it is.

"When Mary's husband Thomas died, they only had one surviving child – a boy called John. Or Ioan in Welsh," Mrs Maddox says. "He probably went to America to seek work because there was no employment to be had locally. I've already told you how hard those times were, but it must have been a big sacrifice for Mary to let him go."

You enter the village of Bryn-crug and Mrs Maddox stops outside a row of interesting old cottages. "That's believed to be Mary's cottage," she says. "The one on the end, but it certainly wasn't as smart then as it is now. This is what Lizzie Rowlands wrote about the cottage when she first went inside and met Mary Jones."

Seeing her in such a poor place, the poorest place I have ever seen, made quite an impression on me. She sat in a low chair, near a very small fire, an earthen floor, two three-legged stools, a small round table, a candlestick and a rush candle, and a few matches.'

You look at the cottage. The sun comes out from behind the clouds, and although the front is in shadow, the sun is reflected brightly from a white building opposite, bringing the old cottage to life. You see it as a picture of God flooding his light onto a place where an old woman once lived in poverty to serve him.

"Mary Jones lived upstairs in her old age, with her niece Lydia Williams helping her," Mrs Maddox explains. "Lydia lived downstairs. By the end of her life Mary was blind, and often suffered from serious depression. Lizzie Rowlands, who was only young, would try to cheer Mary up by talking about the old days and the special services in Bala that Mary had been to with other Methodists."

"Did Mary lose her Christian faith?" you ask, horrified.

Mrs Maddox shakes her head. "Mary wasn't at all well, and there *were* times when she was afraid her faith wouldn't hold. So Lizzie Rowlands would say, 'I was taught at Bala that faith would be a comfort, and would uphold me in my old age. But if that's the sort of thing it is, I would prefer not to have it!' Then Lizzie says Mary would get agitated and shout out, 'Oh yes, it's worth having,' with tears running down her thin, grey cheeks. 'Keep seeking it, my dear young girl. I would have nothing, if I did not have this to lean on.'"

This makes you feel better.

"Mary died four days after Christmas in 1864,

so she was just 80," Mrs Maddox explains. "She still had her Bible from Bala, and she read it every day before she became blind. She read it right through four times, and learnt chapters and chapters of it by heart. So when she was blind she had much to fall back on."

Four times? Even reading the whole Bible once is impressive!

"When Lydia died, Mary went to live with one of the chapel members. A chapel elder said to her when she was dying, 'You think you'll go to heaven, don't you, Mary Jones?'"

Your heart is in your mouth, wondering what Mary will say. Is it possible for someone to *know* they're going to heaven?

What do you think Mary Jones's answer will be? What would *your* answer be if someone asked *you* the same question?

Mrs Maddox smiles when she sees your face. "Don't worry. Even though Mary Jones was so unwell, she said, **'Yes, I believe I shall go there. But I don't know how on earth they'll put up with me there!'**"

You burst out laughing. This sounds exactly like the Mary Jones you've been imagining.

"Do you feel up to visiting Mary's grave?" Mrs Maddox asks. "I can promise you it's not at all gloomy."

You agree to have a look at it. Capel Bethlehem, the large Calvinistic Methodist chapel, is a short walk away. It has the date 1883 above the door, so the building was only a year old when Mary died. In that case, she would never have been well enough to worship here.

A sign outside says *Bedd Mary Jones*, and below it the translation, *Mary Jones' Grave*.

"Surely the Welsh part of it should give her name as Mari," you say, remembering what you saw on the monument at Mary's Jones's cottage, *Ty'n-y-ddôl*.

Mrs Maddox shrugs. "Maybe her name was always spelt Mary. That's the only way it's spelt in the records, and in her Bible. But there *are* some mistakes that you're going to find here."

You're intrigued, and follow Mrs Maddox through a small gate onto a path that goes round to the back of the chapel. Here you find a lot of graves, mostly marked with slate headstones.

"There's Mary's grave," Mrs Maddox says, pointing up the slope to a grave surrounded by low iron railings.

The headstone is made from a tall piece of black polished granite. It's one of the most impressive graves here.

There's a large, engraved stone tablet in Welsh and English lying flat inside the railings, which Mrs Maddox says was once the main headstone. You read it.

MARY, WIDOW OF THOMAS LEWIS, WEAVER, BRYNCRUG, WHO DIED DEC. 28, 1864, AGED 82.

It goes on to say that she was:

THE WELSH GIRL WHO WALKED FROM ABERGYNOLWYN TO BALA IN 1800 WHEN 16 YEARS OF AGE.

"Can you spot *four* mistakes on the flat stone?" Mrs Maddox asks.

(In case you find it difficult to read the words in the picture on the next page, the words with the four mistakes are in the two paragraphs in capital letters on this page.)

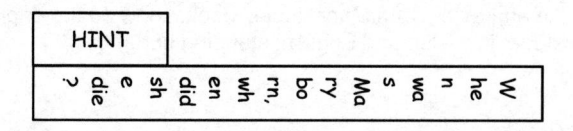

HINT

When was Mary born, when did she die?

An engraving from Mary Ropes' book, showing the original memorial stone, in Welsh and English, standing upright.

Mary Jones's grave today, with the polished black headstone. The old stone now lies flat within the railings that surround the grave.

Calling Mary's husband Thomas Lewis instead of Thomas Jones isn't a mistake, because Mrs Maddox has already explained that's how he was always known. Then you get it. **Mary was 80, not 82** when she died at the end of December 1864, and she was 80 by only a few days. And Mrs Maddox has already told you that **Mary died on the 29th of December, not the 28th**. Also, **Mary walked to Bala from Llanfihangel-y-Pennant, not from Abergynolwyn**. You notice the fourth mistake on both stones. They say **Mary Jones was 16 when she walked to Bala, but she was 15**.

"Didn't anyone check their facts before they cut things into monuments?" you ask in surprise, remembering the mistakes Mrs Maddox has shown you along the way, and the wrong date you spotted on the plaque on Thomas Charles's house in Bala.

"I don't think people saw dates and ages as anything too important," she says. "It's only nowadays, when people have started searching through old records, that exact dates are vital. And without those records it wouldn't really matter . . . would it?"

She's right. The story of Mary Jones would still be the story of Mary Jones, even with the dates and ages a year or two out. "But how many Bibles do you think Mary Jones got in Bala?" you ask.

"It's certainly a puzzle," Mrs Maddox agrees. "Bigger than any puzzle you've been trying to solve this holiday. Lizzie Rowlands says that when Mary reached Bala, Mr Charles sold her three Bibles for the price of one. She brought them home and gave one to her aunt. Some people think her son John took the third copy to America. But the Bibles were all promised to others. So why would Mr Charles be willing to let three go when Mary arrived?"

"Perhaps she told Thomas Charles about her aunt and her son," you suggest.

"But Mary was only fifteen. She had no son. Lizzie Rowlands wrote that Mary had saved up almost five times more than she needed because she had no idea that Mr Charles was selling Bibles so cheaply. The Peter Williams Bible of 1770 cost seventeen shillings, but Mr Charles's Bibles from the SPCK only cost three shillings and sixpence."

"So she bought just one extra one, and gave it to her aunt," you suggest.

"Possibly. In which case, there's no mystery about a missing third Bible. Mary's Bible, as we know, is now in Cambridge, and her aunt's is safely in Aberystwyth."

"Is that what happened?"

Mrs Maddox shakes her head. "I don't think we'll ever know. As we've seen, the problem with some Victorian writers is that they didn't consider the details as important – as long as the story was more or less true. But I've got a theory that fits just about everything."

What do you think her theory is?

"Of course, it's only a theory," Mrs Maddox says, as you walk back through the little gate to the car. "I'm wondering if Thomas Charles sold Mary Jones one Bible at the time, and delivered another one, or perhaps two, to Mary next time he was visiting Llanfihangel-y-Pennant. More Welsh Bibles were coming from London, so he might have been getting spare copies that were not yet promised. He may, or may not, have charged Mary for these."

That's good. It seems to account for all the different stories, assuming each one became slightly muddled with the telling and retelling.

One of your next tasks will be to persuade your Mum and Dad to take you to Cambridge to see the Bible that Mary Jones carried back from Bala in her wallet, walking barefoot to save her precious clogs.

Mrs Maddox has brought her copy of Mary Ropes' 1882 book on Mary Jones. "Mary Ropes can't have known that Mary Jones's father died when she was only four, and she comes up with all sorts of imaginary conversations he had with Mary. Mary Ropes obviously did it to make the story more interesting, but it's very misleading. Of course, Mary Jones's mother may have married again, but I can't find any evidence that she did. Perhaps Mary Ropes heard about an uncle or neighbour who supported Mary and her mother, and thought it was Mary Jones's father. So the conversations may not have been so imaginary after all.

"Mary Ropes tells the story of Mary's 'father'

making a box for her to keep her savings in, and there may well have been a box that someone made. I think that Mary Ropes couldn't find any record of Mary's father going to chapel, and thought he must have been too ill to go. So she invented some things about him to make the story a bit longer."

Mrs Maddox shows you a picture of Bryn-crug in the same book, which seems to exaggerate the mountains. One thing you're sure of: if you ever write about Mary Jones, you're not going to make anything up!

On the way back to Llanfihangel-y-Pennant you ask Mrs Maddox if someone can really *know* they've been good enough for heaven, or if they have to *hope* they've been good enough to get in. You think Mary Jones must have been good enough, because it was partly through her that the Bible Society was founded.
What do *you* think?

Mrs Maddox smiles. "**Yes, Mary knew** – not because of all the good things she'd done, because *no one* is good enough. It was because she trusted Jesus. Jesus says in John 6, verse 37, 'I will never turn away anyone who comes to me.' And that means *you*, as well as Mary Jones, no matter what you've done!"

Well, your time in Llanfihangel-y-Pennant is coming to an end today. You walk down the lane after breakfast for one last look at the old stone bridge and *Ty'n-y-ddôl*, Mary Jones's cottage. There's even time for a quick expedition up into the woods by the church to see *Y Llechwedd* again, the farmhouse where Mary walked to with her mother.

The Church of St Michael is open, so you have a final look inside to see the exhibition in the vestry. It seems a long time ago now that you first came in here and found the clue that led you to the little red postbox. Well, you've certainly learnt a lot about Mary Jones since then.

You look at the photograph of Mary Jones's baptism registration. It makes everything seem so real. It says:

<blockquote>
*19th of December Mary
Daughter of Jacob Jones a
Peasant Mary his Wife 1784.*
</blockquote>

On December the 19th, it must have been freezing cold here in the church, and Mary was only three days old! You wonder why Mary's father's employment is given as "a peasant", when he was a weaver. Or were all manual workers classed as peasants at that time in Wales? You'd love to turn detective and crack the mysteries that Mrs Maddox mentioned. Most of the contradictions in dates and ages seem fairly easy to sort out, or dismiss as unimportant mistakes. However, there may well be documents and records hidden away somewhere that could open more doors, and bring long lost information to life.

You'd especially like to find out exactly how many Bibles Mary had from the Rev'd Thomas Charles. Because if there were three, the third one might still be around somewhere. In America? Here in Wales? On a market stall in Bala? Now, that really *would* be a treasure to find!

When you get back to *Ty'n-y-mynydd* your parents have loaded the car and are waiting for you. Mrs Maddox hands you a piece of paper. "Something to think about over the next few days," she says, with a wink. "And I've given your parents some sandwiches to keep the wolf from the door!"

> ABOUT YOUR MOST ENJOYED
> ADVENTURE
> WHAT YOU HAVE?

1878

But before you solve that puzzle, try this one! Here is an old engraving that is supposed to be of Mary Jones, made from a photograph. She is holding her precious Bible. The original photograph is missing, so all we have now is this engraving first published in *Sunday at Home* in 1878 and again in the book by Mary Ropes' (MER) published in 1882, plus the different picture on the next page from Mary Ropes' book which was republished in 1894. In those days, the person being photographed was told they must sit absolutely still for several seconds and look serious, so it's not surprising if she looks a bit glum.

It's likely that Mary Ropes' publishers looked at the photograph again in 1894, thought it was a bit scary, and had this new one made. However, in 1910 Lizzie Rowlands wrote in a letter that the person in the original photograph was an old lady from Dolgellau who was dressed up to be like Mary, but looked nothing like her! Mary Jones only became famous after her death, and may never have been photographed. But that doesn't mean this second picture isn't like Mary Jones, because someone who had known her could have described her to the new artist. What do you think? Please don't ask Mrs Maddox. She has no idea at all!

The paper Mrs Maddox gave you says: **What have you enjoyed most about your adventure?** The answer to that, of course, is up to you. You can easily find Llanfihangel-y-Pennant on internet sites like Google Earth and Google Images, but you need to include Tywyn in your search name as there are two Llanfihangel-y-Pennants in Wales. Maybe you would like to visit this part of Wales. If so, here are some helpful directions.

Mary Jones's cottage *Ty'n-y-ddôl* is about half a mile (1km) beyond Saint Michael's Church in Llanfihangel-y-Pennant, (Llanfihangel means the Church of Saint Michael), by the small bridge over the river. It is clearly marked when you get there. There is a permanent exhibition about Mary Jones inside Saint Michael's Church. In the churchyard, the grave of Mary's parents is on the left just beyond the main doorway. It is marked by the small slate headstone shown in this book.

Opposite the church is a footpath leading up into the woods, and it's a short walk to the dilapidated farmhouse of *Y Llechwedd*. There are several large chapels in Abergynolwyn, but the original Cwrt Calvinistic Methodist chapel used by Mary and her mother is down by the river, and has been converted into two cottages. Mary is buried at Capel Bethlehem at Bryn-crug. The grave is large, up the slope, and very noticeable.

If Mary Jones had a third Bible, I certainly don't know where it is! Do you? Good hunting!

Epilogue

Mary Jones was just one of many people of all ages who walked long distances to Bala, anxious to get a Bible from Thomas Charles. But her story was an important link in a chain that led to the founding of the British and Foreign Bible Society, though certainly not the only link. Nor, of course, was Thomas Charles the only person involved in the founding of the Society.

So what marks Mary out as a special person? It is this. For more than two hundred years her story has been told countless times, inspiring young people to give themselves to God's work – when they realize that God needs and uses ordinary people.

The Bible Mary gave to her aunt is in the National Library of Wales in Aberystwyth. Her own Bible is in the Cambridge University Library, showing considerable signs of wear and tear from heavy use. If you want to see either of these, you have to arrange a viewing in advance with the libraries.

If you would like to find out more about the Bible and the Christian faith, you can contact Bible Society (http://www.biblesociety.org.uk), or talk with your church minister or a Christian friend. And that's when the adventure *really* begins!

AGATHOS, THE ROCKY ISLAND,
AND OTHER STORIES
Chris Wright

ISBN 978-0-9525956-8-7
White Tree Publishing

Once upon a time there were two favorite books for Sunday reading: *Parables From Nature* and *Agathos and The Rocky Island*.

These books contained all sorts of short stories, usually with a hidden meaning. In this illustrated book is a selection of the very best of these stories, carefully retold to preserve the feel of the originals, coupled with ease of reading and understanding for today's readers.

Discover the king who sent his servants to trade in a foreign city; the butterfly who thought her eggs would hatch into baby butterflies; and the two boys who decided to explore the forbidden land beyond the castle boundary. The spider that kept being blown in the wind; the soldier who had to fight a dragon; the four children who had to find their way through a dark and dangerous forest. These are just six of the nine stories in this collection. Oh, and there's also one about a rocky island!

This is a book for a young person to read alone; a family or parent to read aloud; Sunday school teachers to read to the class; and even for grownups who want to dip into the fascinating stories of the past all by themselves. Can you discover the hidden meanings? You don't have to wait until Sunday before starting!

5.5 x 8.5 inches 148 pages £5.95
Available from major internet stores

PILGRIM'S PROGRESS
AN ADVENTURE BOOK
Chris Wright

ISBN: 978-0-9525956-6-3
White Tree Publishing

Travel with young Christian as he sets out on a difficult and perilous journey to find the King. Solve the puzzles and riddles along the way, and help Christian reach the Celestial City. Then travel with his friend Christiana. She has four young brothers who can sometimes be a bit of a problem.

Be warned, you will meet giants and lions – and even dragons! There are people who don't want Christian and Christiana to reach the city of the King and his Son. But not everyone is an enemy. There are plenty of friendly people. It's just a matter of finding them.

Are you prepared to help? Are you sure? The journey can be very dangerous! As with this book about Mary Jones, you can enjoy the story even if you don't want to try the puzzles.

This is a book with a story containing a mix of puzzles. The suggested reading age is up to ten or eleven. Older readers will find the same story told in much greater detail in *Pilgrim's Progress — Special Edition*, without the puzzles.

5.5 x 8.5 inches 174 pages £6.95
Available from major internet stores

PILGRIM'S PROGRESS
SPECIAL EDITION
Chris Wright
ISBN: 978-0-9525956-7-0
White Tree Publishing

This book for all ages will be a great favourite with young readers, as well as with families, Sunday school teachers, and anyone who wants to read John Bunyan's *Pilgrim's Progress* in a clear form.

All the old favourites are here: Christian, Christiana, the Wicket Gate, Interpreter, Hill Difficulty with the lions, the four sisters at the House Beautiful, Vanity Fair, Giant Despair, Faithful and Talkative – and, of course, Greatheart. The list is almost endless.

The first part of the story is told by Christian himself, as he leaves the City of Destruction to reach the Celestial City, and becomes trapped in the Slough of Despond near the Wicket Gate. On his journey he will encounter lions, giants, and a creature called the Destroyer.

Christiana follows along later, and tells her own story in the second part. Not only does Christiana have to cope with her four young brothers, she worries about whether her clothes are good enough for meeting the King. Will she find the dangers in Vanity Fair that Christian found? Will she be caught by Giant Despair and imprisoned in Doubting Castle? What about the dragon with seven heads?

It's a dangerous journey, but Christian and Christiana both know that the King's Son is with them, helping them through the most difficult parts until they reach the Land of Beulah, and see the Celestial City on the other side of the Dark River. This is a story you will remember for ever, and it's about a journey you can make for yourself.

5.5 x 8.5 inches 278 pages £8.95
Available from major internet stores

ZEPHAN AND THE VISION

Chris Wright

ISBN: 978-0-9525956-9-4
White Tree Publishing

An exciting story about the adventures of two angels who seem to know almost nothing – until they have a vision!

Two ordinary angels are caring for the distant Planet Eltor, and they are about to get a big shock – they are due to take a trip to the Planet Earth! This is Zephan's story of the vision he is given before being allowed to travel with Talora, his companion angel, to help two young people fight against the enemy.

Arriving on Earth, they discover that everyone lives in a small castle. Some castles are strong and built in good positions, while others appear weak and open to attack. But it seems that the best-looking castles are not always the most secure.

Meet Castle Nadia and Castle Max, the two castles that Zephan and Talora have to defend. And meet the nasty creatures who have built shelters for themselves around the back of these castles. And worst of all, meet the shadow angels who live in a cave on Shadow Hill. This is a story about the forces of good and the forces of evil. Who will win the battle for Castle Nadia?

The events in this story are based very loosely on John Bunyan's allegory *The Holy War*.

5.5 x 8.5 inches 216 pages £7.95
Available from major internet stores

Lightning Source UK Ltd.
Milton Keynes UK
UKOW040641010812

196872UK00001B/49/P